Cover Image Credit/Copyright Attribution: IIIerlok_Xolms/Shutterstock

Nocturnal Fabulations

Ecology, Vitality and Opacity in the Cinema of Apichatpong Weerasethakul

Érik Bordeleau, Toni Pape, Ronald Rose-Antoinette and Adam Szymanski

With an introduction by Erin Manning

Open Humanities Press is an international, scholar-led open access publishing collective whose mission is to make leading works of contemporary critical
thought freely available worldwide. More at http://openhumanitiespress.org

Contents

Erin Manning

Introduction

> Intercessors are essential. Creation is all about
> intercessors. Without them, there is no work.
> *Gilles Deleuze (1995: 125, translation modified)*

When the Immediations book series at Open Humanities Press
was launched, it was done with Gilles Deleuze's concept of the
intercessor[1] in mind. We were looking for a way to give voice to
a kind of collaboration that would work from within the weave
of research and writing, a collaboration that would give texture
to a voice (or a multiplicity of voice) toward a conversation to
come. A conversation to come is one that invents interlocutors,
one that refuses to know in advance where the encounter will
lead. Deleuze calls this a minoritarian discourse: "We must catch
someone fabulating, catch them 'in the act' of fabulating. Then a
minoritarian discourse, with two or many speakers, takes shape…
To catch fabulation in the act is to seize the movement of the
constitution of a people. A people never preexists (translation
modified)" (Deleuze 1995: 125–6).

*Nocturnal Fabulations: Ecology, Vitality and Opacity in the Cinema
of Apichatpong Weerasethakul*, an eight-handed, four-bodied book
by Érik Bordeleau, Ronald Rose-Antoinette, Toni Pape and Adam
Szymanski, is an essay in intercessing. This is not a book that is
simply "about" the work of the cinematographer Apichatpong

Weerasethakul, though it does engage his work in detail. It is a book that deeply questions *what else* might be at stake in setting up the conditions for collaboration across two genres – cinema and writing. It is a book that asks *what else* this uneasy interstice of image-thought can look like when it moves onto the page. This thinking-with can be understood as an engagement with how the films of Apichatpong themselves propose collective ecologies of thought and how these ecologies foreground new ways of seeing the image as a movement of thought. This gesture of thinking with and across image and text, of being moved by a work that intercesses two discrete but intertwined perceptual processes, developing vocabulary not to "explain" the work but to reactivate it by other means, proposes a wholly different ethos of engagement. Refusing to position itself outside Apichatpong's work in an effort to situate it once and for all within a genre, or within a historical period, or order it using a theoretical method, what *Nocturnal Fabulations* proposes instead is a direct engagement with the forces of thought that move through the work and make it work. It is an attempt, in writing, to see *where else* these forces can lead. Apichatpong Weerasethakul is a perfect match for such a project: there is always a sense, in watching his films, that he is a participant in a process that has yet to quite unfold, and that his work is, before all else, dedicated to a people (and a conversation) yet to come.

Apichatpong describes his work as "open cinema", and often seems at odds with questions interviewers pose, uneasy with their probing into plot sequence and intentionality: "Sometimes you don't need to understand everything to appreciate a certain beauty," he tells one interviewer. "And I think the film operates in the same way. It's like tapping into someone's mind. The thinking pattern is quite random, jumping here and there like a monkey" (Rose 2010). In another interview: "I believe that cinema has its own life," and then, when the interviewer prods a bit more: "Yeah, but the more I explain, the more the movie loses its mystery so I think I should stop! [...] [I]t's the mood and the feeling that matters to me" (Peranson 2010).

With some filmmakers, one might have the sense of these being anti-intellectual attempts to avoid taking a stance – "you just have to feel it – as I can't explain it" a stand-in for "the artist has an intuition that comes from outside the everyday and defies explanation." This is not what is at stake with Apichatpong, for his films do always take a stance, and he does not shy away from complex conceptual-aesthetic issues. But he does trouble language, especially the kind of language that would like to frame experience, his effort more directed toward the complexity of what feeling can do at the edges of ineffability. Here feeling is not so much outside of language as *with* its uneasy telling, the plot not carried by the tenor of an emotion that orients the image as by the affective tonality of a thinking-feeling that resists stable time signatures. Language is made uneasy precisely because it does not easily speak in the cacophony of time unmoored. What is felt in Apichatpong's work, what matters in the feeling, is carried forth by an image that cannot quite be left behind in the explaining. To explain the work, to categorize it sequentially, as interviewers (and critics) are wont to do, is to misunderstand how its movements undermine any kind of linear telling. It is to underestimate what the image can do.

There is great richness in what is carried forth in Apichatpong's work, and it is this that the texts that follow embrace. In this sense, theirs can also be imagined as a kind of futurist archeological work, a speculative gesture not of this time that touches the limits of *what else* the image can do, asking, with Apichatpong, what it might mean to think like a monkey jumps.

To be an intercessor is to attend to the qualities of the thresholds of an encounter between forces and forms of thought, and to inquire, each time anew, how the threshold carries incipient form from image to experience, from experience to image.

For how we perceive really matters in Apichatpong's works: "everything matters, [...] you're not really looking forward to the finished work but looking forward to every moment; enjoying every moment" (Elphick 2015). What is unusual, however, is that this mattering isn't primarily inward-looking: the image's thinking-feeling does not begin and end here, in this cinematic experiment, in this plot sequence.

> Before I used to think of film as maybe just one
> project. With my process being finishing it piece
> by piece, before moving on to different themes
> or interests. But lately I think of film like satellites:
> surrounding this ongoing universe; even building that
> universe. So when I finished *Cemetery of Splendour*,
> it wasn't really finished. It's almost like a platform,
> to move onto another work that can be built from
> it. But it all ends up being one piece; all together".
> (Elphick 2015)

Open cinema as punctually expressed singularity across a series that cannot be reduced to the sum of its parts. Open cinema as relational platform across times in the cinematic making.

To be an intercessor is to *participate* in this relational platform, not to *mediate* it. It is to recognize how the immediacy of an encounter with an image, with a movement of thought, or better yet, with the intervals of thought-images yet to come, affects what it means to perceive. Intercessors change the norms of contact. Changing the norms of contact is always a creative gesture: there is no intercessor that would exist once and for all, nor is there a creative act that can flourish without intercession. "Fictive or real, animated or inanimate, one must make one's intercessors. It is a series. If you don't form a series, even completely imaginary, you are lost. I need my intercessors to express myself, and they would never be able to express themselves without me: we are always many at work, even when you don't see it" (Deleuze 1995: 125, translation modified).

To act is to have been intercessed, to have been moved by conditions beyond the frame of an encounter predetermined. A creative act, it must be underscored, is not something that belongs to me: the work is activated in a field of relation that is always lively with intercessions. And so to seek to know a work is to be curious about how it has been intercessed.

Intercession occurs at all levels: the artist is intercessor, the writer is intercessor, the ecologies that orient their coming together are intercessing. In the case of Apichatpong, the intercessions are wildly layered: histories that refuse to remain unspoken, tales retold in settings too strange to serve as placeholders for simple ideological positioning, characters (re)emerging from future-pasts, haunting the image that itself refuses to stand still. It is the complexity of intercession that keeps the image moving: the creative impulse is no longer restrained to that which flies off the screen today into the movie theatre or tomorrow into the textual analysis. Intercessions move through Apichatpong's films, activating cinema's potential for coming-between in times as yet uncharted.

Toni Pape, Ronald Rose-Antoinette, Adam Szymanski and Érik Bordeleau tend to this perception-in-act. "The feeling of a story exceeds the hard facts of its plot and outlasts its delivery," writes Toni Pape in this collection (20). What else can the image do, he wonders, in the intervals of its own becoming, a time he calls "no-longer-not-yet: no longer street vendor, not yet storyteller; no longer documentary, not yet fiction"? (Pape, this collection: 23) What fabulations, Pape asks, can operate in the seriality of an image-time that defies chronology while not resisting strong moments of representation, a time of consistency more than of coherence? *What else* can populate the living screen when "cinema creates an opening in life and gives us a chance to fabulate a detour, to meander along life's indirect ways?" (Pape, this collection: 30)

These open questions are everywhere present in this book that engages in a very close reading of Apichatpong's work without ever forgetting that the action of pinning-it-down threatens to weaken the intercessory collaboration. For to know is not to intercess but to settle into position. How might writing alter what else is happening here, each author seems to wonder, how might writing follow the detours invited by the images? How might writing further the thinking-feeling that opens the image – the cinema – to its outside at every turn? How might it create intercrossings that themselves become invitations for intercessors to come? *How else* might the conversation take place between mediums so potentially incompatible as the temporality of the image undone and undoing, and the words relacing and knotting?

But, their writing also suggests: wouldn't it be unwise to underestimate the power of words, and to miss the force of what a gesture of intercession that moves between language and image can compose? In this book which presents itself in both English and French – a book written across two languages and discussed always in the crossing of these languages, read and re-read by its authors with the kind of attention that retains the singularity of each contribution even as it suggests a practice of collective writing – the potentials are many, including the potential of language to activate the force of what an image can do when it gives itself over to the text.

A collective writing doesn't have to be four-bodied at each turn. Like the becoming-image, like the movement of thought, it can be an across-ness, a punctual gesturing toward a collective project that refuses to succumb to a oneness of perspective. This gesture is similar to what Adam Szymanski sees in Apichatpong's films when he discusses their ecological reach – ecological not only in the sense of their reverence for nature, but equally in their concern for how an ecology is co-inhabited by a range of different beings usually separated by the divisions built up between humans and non-humans and between the living and the dead. An engagement with an ecological approach to image-thought, or what Szymanski calls an "ecosophic aesthetic" is one that recognizes the taut and elastic connections between tendencies in an evolving environment. An ecosophic aesthetic hones techniques for perceiving more closely the forces that compose and dissolve a community, those forces that make felt the undercurrents of existence as we know it. These forces are everywhere present in Apichatpong's work – they are what detours the story, what prevents the plot from giving itself too easily to the curious interviewer.

These forces, I want to suggest, are also active in the listening-across of these four texts. As are the detourings. The collectivity of the writing is more ecological, more ecosophically aesthetic, than it is univocal. Resonances are there, but they are there more in force than in form: these four texts do not cite one another, or even necessarily engage with the same films. Sometimes their views have a quality of divergence that differentiates them at a level that language can't quite pinpoint. Something more complex than agreement is at stake – a curiosity, perhaps, with what travels with the words, with the unsaid and its power of articulation. For, like Apichatpong's images, the words that intercess must also carry a certain uneasiness with recognition. They must also trouble the tendency to be held in place.

But how to begin when forces are everywhere active in an aesthetic ecosophy? This is Ronald Rose-Antoinette's question and the refrain that moves his text. The answer is simple: in the middle. This is not a simple task, however, constrained as we are by language's tendency to place thought subjectly-verbly-objectly in a row. Language must break, must almost reach its absolute resistance, and here, perhaps, the image's potential will be felt.

Fig. 1: The close-up of the monkey-ghost looking straight at us with his red eyes, from *Uncle Boonmee Who Can Recall His Past Lives*.

The image's potential, Rose-Antoinette suggests, recasts what memory can be. In Apichatpong's work, a memory is crafted that troubles an account of recognition. This is not a memory for that which is known, for a past contained. It is a memory of a futurity, a memory of a trace. A future "unforgettable" (Rose-Antoinette, this collection: 125).

An image of the future. With monkeys lurking, unsettling both thought and image, bringing language to its limit. But that's the point: that the image refuses to stand still, even when at its most still, as when the camera encounters the monkey-ghost looking straight at us with his red eyes.

We are haunted by the red eyes, haunted by the magic lantern that keeps us in the atemporality of an image that refuses to settle. We are "called" as Rose-Antoinette writes in this collection, "to err into a future" that is more orientation than goal. No film of Apichatpong ever leaves us with a sense of knowing what comes next (or even what has come to pass). Time errs and takes us into that erring.

An allure is present, a style. This is Érik Bordeleau's contribution. "For the word 'allure' points toward the singular manner that courses through a being and characterizes it, a sort of evanescent signature – a style – charged with a force of affective propulsion that invites further folds and relays" (Bordeleau, this collection: 80). The image seduces us, but it also causes a certain disquiet. It moves slowly, the takes often long, the visuals strangely more-than real. Of this place and yet beyond. An uneasiness lurks even while we feel ourselves pulled in, caught up, a lure for feeling taking over that disorients, that calls attention toward itself in a way that exceeds expectation. We watch in ways unaccustomed. We are made uneasy by the way the image errs, and we are moved in this erring.

When Deleuze says we must invent our own intercessors, what he also means is that we are never wholly ourselves. Apichatpong provides a window into this unseemliness and invites us to linger here, to be engaged in what matters via the image, via its magic lanterning – the history of Thailand, its repression, the role of death in experience, the place of sickness, and of dreams, the relation of animal and human worlds, the environmental crisis – without providing a sense of where to go or who to be. For that is not the work of the image. It is not the image's work to narrate where the process can go. The film is a platform, and as a platform, it will only ever be as good as its intercessors. What the image can do matters, but its mattering moves far beyond where the image-as-content can go. The image-mattering must call intercessors into the act.

This is also true of writing. The writing with an artwork can only ever do its work if it proposes operations that exceed its bounds.

The condition of a people to come, as Deleuze might say, is that the work always remains to be done.

The cinema of Apichatpong Weerasethakul needs to be acted. It needs to be dreamed. "Thus cinema can be a phantom in this sense: because it's something that you really need to dream. Cinema is a vehicle we produce for ourselves and as part of us. It's like an extension of our soul that manifests itself" (Kim cited in Bordeleau, this collection: 90). It needs to be dreamed not to unravel its content, but to create more capacity to dream, to explore what Bordeleau calls the "unprecedented degrees of defocalisation that Apichatpong manages to operate directly on the subtle element [that is cinema]" (Bordeleau, this collection: 90).

Apichatpong's films make us visionaries. This is perhaps their first act of intercession. In doing so, they force us to ask not what we've seen, but what we have not yet been able to see. And they invite us to see it with the eyes of an other, more-than real, more-than human.

Notes

1. It is important to note that the English translation speaks of "mediators" when Deleuze writes of "intercessors". Intercessors are the opposite of mediators: they don't move between already-identifiable terms. They create the terms of their eventual intercession. They are immediators.

Works Cited

Deleuze, Gilles. *Negotiations. 1972–1990.* New York: Columbia University Press, 1995.

Elphick, Jeremy. "Cemetery of Splendour – An Interview with Apichatpong Weerasethakul." *4:3 Film.* Published on October 22, 2015.

Available from: http://fourthreefilm.com/2015/10/cemetery-of-splendour-an-interview-with-apichatpong-weerasethakul/ (accessed on June 17, 2016).

Rose, Steve. "'You Don't Have to Understand Everything': Apichatpong Weerasethakul." *The Guardian*. Published November 11, 2010. Available from: https://www.theguardian.com/film/2010/nov/11/apichatpong-weerasethakul-director-uncle-boonmee-interview (accessed on June 17, 2016).

Peranson, Mark. "Ghost in the Machine: Apichatpong Weerasethakul's Letter to Cinema." *CinemaScope* 43 (2010). Available from: http://cinema-scope.com/spotlight/spotlight-ghost-in-the-machine-apichatpong-weerasethakuls-letter-to-cinema/ (accessed on June 17, 2016).

What is a "mode of life"? A first, rather technical attempt at an answer might come to the term mode from the perspective of grammar. We would then think of a mode (often also "mood") as a grammatical marker that expresses one's attitude towards a statement. Do we express a fact, an order, a possibility, a desire? Accordingly, we would speak (at least in the few Indo-European languages that we know) in the indicative, imperative, conditional or subjunctive moods. And, indeed, one can live by "facts" and order-words. Or one can live by potentials and desires.

Such a technical approach lends itself to diffuse a bit the grandeur that one might attribute to the expression "modes of life". For starters, nobody lives in only one mode just like nobody speaks in just one grammatical mode. The potentiality of the "maybe" in its pure form would be as unlivable as the oppressive determination of a continuous imperative. A life is composed through the interplay of various modes. (In other words, a mode of life is not a "way of life".) So with respect to the cinema of Apichatpong this means that there is no single, definitive mode of life we could ascribe to him as the "auteur". Rather, his films create moods or tonalities that infuse our lived reality and can inflect our lines of life.

The second point then is that modes of life are minor forces that can act temporarily. If we expect a film to "completely change our life" we are bound to be disappointed. But if we can think of change on a microscopic scale, then we can begin to register the minor inflections produced by the mood of a film. The force of *Mysterious Object at Noon* consists precisely in infusing people's everyday life with the unassuming "what if" of fabulation, making way for so many other "maybes". A similar thing happens in *The Adventures of Iron Pussy* when we co-perform new (minor) genders with the image. That, to us, is a mode/mood of life. And thought in this sense, Apichatpong's cinema opens up the possibility for new modes of life.

One more word about what is "new" about them because that is of course another grand word. Many of Apichatpong's films deal in one way or another with the history of Thailand. Now, in what mode does cinema usually stage the encounter with history? Mainly in the factual mode of the indicative. Think of Hollywood's historical dramas and their obsession with realism as well as a very conservative notion of mimetic "method" acting. Or think of the many documentaries which, even if they re-write history, tell us "how it really was". (Of course, there are numerous interesting exceptions.) It is in this context that Apichatpong's cinema really makes a difference, proposing an encounter with history in the conditional and subjunctive modes, asking not only what could have happened but also how the past could still be acting today, asking what the past desires. One interesting thing that happens when you infuse history with the "maybe" of the conditional is that time stops being linear. This is what the chapter on *Mysterious Object at Noon* and *Iron Pussy* suggests when it talks about concurring re-tellings of the past. Somebody who says "Oh, let me tell the story. You've got it all wrong!" is effectively recreating a mood that is bound to shape the present moment. The past, as it is now experienced in retrospect, really was different. In a similar way, Apichatpong's films productively falsify one another across time, ultimately making chronology a rather useless concept. There is no chronological beginning or end to Apichatpong's oeuvre. There is beginning only in the sense that we give to it (following Nietzsche and Guattari) of cosmic emergence or eternal return. A beginning that is always in the present.

Toni Pape

The Vitality of Fabulation: Improvisation and Clichés in *Mysterious Object at Noon* and *The Adventure of Iron Pussy*

The Feeling of a Story

Let's begin with a cliché: everybody enjoys a good story.

From here, one may go on and ask what constitutes a story. Or one could continue and dispute the contentious criteria that make for a *good* story. Either way, one has already moved to the end of the sentence. What if one lingers in the proposition, general though it may be? We may, in that case, discover a concern with joy. We may even encounter a collectivity cloaked as "everybody". Storytelling, even for the solitary writer, is an affair of the many, an experience of the multiple. The telling of a story, of *any* story from family lore to shared mythologies, is a force that, among many other effects, can bind or dissolve a community. You can notice it in the sharing of stories in a family or between friends: "How did you two meet?" or "Remember that prank we played on our history teacher? What was her name again?" And so the ball gets rolling. What unravels from such balls of yarn is not just a sequence of events as related but a *feeling* of past life that colors the present. The feeling of a story exceeds the hard facts of its plot and outlasts its delivery. Think of a novel or a film that affected you as a teenager. Do you remember the story? Somewhat, but hardly. What remains is a feeling, an affective tone which, strictly speaking, you don't even need to remember because it returns effortlessly and wholly, all by itself. The telling of a story, remembered or invented or a bit of both, opens towards a collective dreaming, in which life-*as-is* softens and becomes sensitive to its own potential: life in the mode of *what if*. This mode of the *what-if* suspends the evidentness of the everyday, the routines of the *as-is*, and flushes the moment with the joy of speculation. "What would you do if you won the lottery?" The thrill of this most inconsequential question arises from the opening it creates: for a moment, nothing is obvious, everything could be different. It's not much different for the past. "Oh, let *me* tell the story. You've got it all wrong!" The past could have been different; it depends on the telling. Storytelling makes for joyful speculation because it becomes momentarily possible to reinvent life. This collective feeling spills over the narrative proper and resonates forth into life-living.[1] The cliché's "everybody" is really an anybody in the making.

Fabulation and Joy

Mysterious Object at Noon is a story invented over the duration of three years by various people all across Thailand. The film is shot in black-and-white on 16 mm film, which contributes to a pronounced lo-fi, documentary aesthetic. Inspired by the surrealist procedure called *cadavre exquis*, Apichatpong Weerasethakul – who is credited here as a mere "story editor" – meanders from the northern provinces of Thailand to the south and, in a series of chance encounters, asks street vendors, farmers, local theater groups, and children to collectively tell a story. Each storyteller has to continue the tale where it had been left off. Together, they slowly turn a fairly straightforward exposition into an intricate tale of humans, animals, and aliens.

Fig. 2: Still from *Mysterious Object at Noon*, 16 mm (blown up to 35 mm).

The first shot of the film is from inside a vehicle, a vending truck selling seafood, that makes its way through busy city streets. For minutes, we roam through the urban landscape; a radio soap opera offers a wistful tune on the radio soon accompanied by the voice of a narrator relating a story of love and loss. The vendors have a purpose but no particular destination, roving the neighborhoods to sell their goods at this street corner or another. Open drift and dreamy song set the tone for the next hour and a half or so. We'll never lose this momentum as the camera moves from one storyteller to the next, even as it stands still to record bits of story. As the truck comes to one of its many halts, we meet one of the vendors who becomes the first narrator in the film. She relates her own story: sold by her parents for two bus tickets back to their village home, she now ekes out an existence on the streets of Bangkok. She has barely finished her story when the "editor" behind the camera asks: "Now, do you have any other stories to tell us? It can be real or fiction. [...] Any story ... from a book or something." Tell us any story besides yours. Or rather: now that we have heard your story, tell us something else, something more that isn't you. You + *n*. This is how *Mysterious Object at Noon* passes through the personal into the impersonal, in a continuation of a familiar gesture into the unknown. Continue the telling and extend it into the untold. The vendor hesitates longer than the camera. Before she begins to fabulate, the image already holds the scene: a boy in a wheelchair doing his schoolwork at a desk; a woman stands by the window, her back towards the camera (Fig. 2).

The sound is still that of the busy street corner: "Big tuna fish is coming... tuna fish." What are these images that flash onto the screen unannounced, right out of the bustling street? We could say that, structurally, the image simply precedes the speech-act that will produce it by a few seconds – a stylistic choice. But the specific relation between sound and image brings something else into sensation, which I would call the *incipiency of fabulation* that is also a feeling of potential. For the image of the boy and his teacher does not yet signify the vendor's story; rather, it signals the force of a story forming itself, preparing to cast itself into words. The divide between image and sound gives us a sensation of the fullness of an interval in which everything is allowed to differ from itself, creatively. It is in those few seconds of suspension that the vendor exceeds her role as a "social actor" in a becoming-storyteller, but not without the director's becoming-illustrator and the documentary's becoming-fabulation. In other words, this sequence signals the multiplicity of becoming that *Mysterious Object at Noon* activates. The image can precede its own verbal invention because chronologies of before-and-after do not operate in this interval of becoming. The time of becoming is a no-longer-not-yet: no longer street vendor, not yet storyteller; no longer documentary, not yet fiction.

Eventually, the story comes into language, in voice-over:

> Let's say there was a house. There was a disabled
> boy and a teacher who came to teach him everyday.
> He didn't have a chance to see the outside world.
> So she brought lots of photographs for him to see.

> The boy was happy with a chance to be able to study
> like others. His parents hired his teacher but they
> were never home. But I am happy to see him with a
> good teacher.

Then the street vendor falls silent. The subsequent interactions between the boy and the teacher are rendered in images and intertitles. "What did you do in the outside world today?" he asks her. We see her negotiating for prices on a market. Intertitle: "'Then I had my hair done,' the teacher says." Through the intertitles, the film takes on a new aesthetic consistency, which is not so much that of the silent film era but of the impersonal written word. Again only for a brief moment, language does not belong to anyone. Of course, we can assume that it is still the street vendor who tells the story. Clearly, it is the teacher who says, "I had my hair done." But in both cases, on both levels of narration, the telling of the tale has detached itself from the human body and can appear as a pure enunciative act, as pure experience. This intensity is difficult to sustain. And indeed, *Mysterious Object at Noon* will soon move back towards the personal, at the latest when we encounter the next storyteller-farmer-performer. But impersonality as such is not the goal. *Mysterious Object at Noon* weaves together storytelling as a personal creation and as a pure, impersonal experience in order to unleash the potential of storytelling as a collective invention towards a re-invention of the collective in the process.

This is fabulation. It is a matter of:

> providing [oneself] with 'intercessors,' that is, of taking
> real and not fictional characters, but putting these
> very characters in the condition of 'making up fiction,'
> of 'legending,' of 'fabulating.' The author takes a step
> towards his characters, but the characters take a step
> towards the author: double becoming. Fabulation is
> not an impersonal myth, but neither is it a personal

> fiction: it is a word in act, a speech-act through which
> the character continually crosses the boundary which
> would separate his private business from politics, and
> which *itself produces collective utterances*. (Deleuze
> 1989: 222, translation modified)

Neither personal, nor impersonal. *Collective.* One does not differ from oneself without an intercessor – a human being, a camera, a story – that pries open the habitual frame of the subject and lures one into self-differentiation. By way of these encounters creative of a world, fabulation can count as a mode of living. It opens life to the unknown and tentatively composes a new temporary and liveable constellation. In this sense, fabulation is a catalyst for self-differentiation.

How, then, can we qualify life in the fabulatory mode? It is certainly improvised rather than scripted. The fabulators in *Mysterious Object at Noon* pick up the strands of a story where they have been left off by someone else. It is impossible for them to know what form their tale is going to eventually take. The next storyteller in line might take it and, more or less carefully, turn it into something completely different. If Apichatpong's film resonates with the Surrealists' exquisite corpses, it is through this indetermination of form. Consider the *cadavre exquis, Nude*, collectively drawn by Yves Tanguy, Joan Miró, Max Morise, and Man Ray in 1926 and 1927 (Fig. 3).

The experiment produces a body that is as yet unorganized – a leafy snail-human – that does not yet know how its various parts will function together. And yet it is there, on the page, as a lure for the imagination. This appeal to fabulate can be felt all the more strongly if we consider the process rather than the product. Indeed, the most important aspect of the *cadavre exquis* is not its fabulous outcome but the collective experimentation it requires. You cannot see Tanguy, Miró, Morise, and Man Ray draw this impossible body, but imagine them. Or remember an occasion

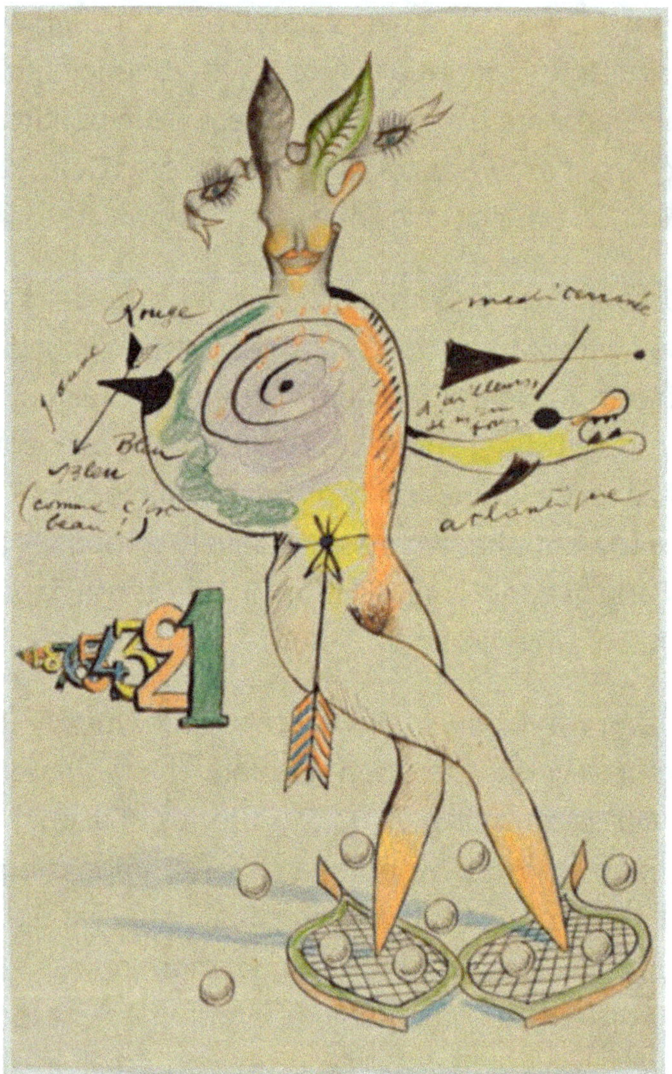

Fig. 3: *Nude*. Cadavre Exquis with Yves Tanguy, Joan Miró, Max Morise, and Man Ray (1926–1927).

on which you've played this game with friends. You pick up the end of a few lines with a minimum of information – the distance between the lines and their direction – and have to continue the drawing. The task involves hesitation and doubt about the figurative content of those lines. All you can do is advance in a speculative mode, that is, continue without knowing what will have taken form. But there is also joy in continuing with a difference, in knowing that you will connect and cut at the same time. Here, as in any improvisation, the first rule is to always say "yes and…". Improvisation harnesses the indetermination of form in an affirmative way, trusting that the leap of faith will land the experiment in a safety net of collective care only to rebound into another moment of suspension.

Mysterious Object at Noon is a series of such affirmative acts, each of which brings out the joyful suspense of the relay. Here is the first such instance in the film. After Apichatpong, the "story editor", has illustrated the beginning of the tale, the street vendor's voice returns:

> While they were studying, the teacher, her name is Dogfahr, left for a restroom. [...] Then he [the boy] became suspicious. Why there was no word from the teacher. He entered the room and saw the teacher lying on the floor. [...] He tried to open the door. He desperately wanted to help her. He dragged her into the room, to the bed. He... He saw... He saw an object rolling out from her skirt... That was very strange.

And cut. We're back in the car. The story – suspended at the cliffhanger moment of the mysterious object rolling out of a skirt – ambulates into the countryside, stopping at a small cottage and a farmer.

> Grandpa, what do you say? They just came in with this... That object must be round-shaped. Can it... Can it turn into a kid? I don't think it can.

> Yes. Anything you want.

> That object was like... It looked like a star. It fell down from the sky and turned into a human. It resided in a boy's body. After around a week or two, that boy woke up. He said "I'm OK, I'm OK. I was just by myself. I can foresee everything. I know my brother and sister but now I'm just a kid. I cannot stay with my mother, my father, or anyone. So I was residing in this floating object.

Hesitation – "can it?" – is followed by a pronounced act of fabulation. The farmer tentatively probes the margin of maneuver and, once certain that the story is open wide, she makes the cut and pulls out the next, quite magical segment of the story. Within the next twenty minutes of the film, the story will have traveled to a group of teenagers who, yes, transform the boy into a doppelgänger of the teacher. The teacher and her double then, yes, vie for a place in the boy's life – a story that is acted out by a theater group. And, yes, then the boy turns into a giant… and the ball of yarn rolls on. Two things stand out in this movement of suspensions and cuts. First, *Mysterious Object at Noon* brings out the fullness of the interval between the storytellers. As we move from one intercessor to the next, the film makes sure to provide enough time for us to consider the story-thus-far, to appreciate how it has come into itself. This appreciation is also a momentary holding of its potential. In those moments of suspension, we feel the present moment *and* everything that could come out of it. We feel this all the more vividly because we also know that somebody, *anybody* really, is going to come along and make the cut. It is this certainty of the next cut that makes the interval vibrate with potential. But what comes out, secondly, is that there is no continuation of the story without the cut. There is no invention, no novelty, no time without the actualization of virtuality. Perhaps one of the storytellers in *Mysterious Object at Noon* is aware of this duplicity when he begins by saying: "My story is not really connected." Not really. But all the more because continuation *depends* on disjunction. The cut *is* the connection.

There is, as I said at the beginning, something joyful in this process. Each new storyteller makes us tremble with giddy anxiety at the prospect of her ruthless intervention in the tale of Dogfahr and the boy. This thrilling commotion builds over the length of the film and reaches its climax towards the end when the story is handed over to a group of schoolchildren. What a risk to take! It's like giving your best china to a bunch of kids to play teatime with. You know you're on the losing end. But, oh, the excitement! Within a few moments, Dogfahr has been eaten by a tiger and the boy has been stabbed by the star child. "That's the end." But then: "He has an idea," says one boy pointing at another. And they start over. After all, it's just a story; we can go back and rewrite it. Renewed time and again, invention can approach chance and practise the necessary cut. Creation by accident. Perhaps it is just a lucky accident that *Mysterious Object at Noon* ends with a group of children. Nietzsche's Zarathustra sings "Let chance come to me, it is innocent as a little child" (Nietzsche 1978: 175, translation modified). Child's play is haphazard and effective at the same time, like a throw of dice: the throw both opens up to an array of possibilities and necessarily reduces them to a single outcome. "The dice which are thrown once are the affirmation of *chance*, the combination which they form on falling is the affirmation of *necessity*" (Deleuze 1986a: 26). We have already encountered the inseparable duo of chance and necessity in the guises of the holding-of-potential and the cut. What the children's unabashed fabulation brings out is the double affirmation of both chance and necessity. "What? The teacher's dead?" Apichatpong, behind the camera, asks in surprise. The response is a resolute "Yes and" which does the boy in as well. But, as we have seen, the end is another beginning. What returns in each affirmation is the joy of inventing in collusion with chance. When improvising, you have to appreciate without being precious: hold the potential, make the cut. Enjoy.

The Stroll and Clichés

If this aimless joy is what holds *Mysterious Object at Noon* together despite its various settings, storytellers, and the long timeframe of the shoot, it gives the film the rigorous vagueness of a stroll, which is so rarely encountered in cinema as in life. Think of it, a good stroll is hard to come by. You really need to want to move *without* any particular destination in mind, content not to know which way you turn at the next corner. The movie theater should be an ideal space for this. After all, we commit a considerable stretch of time to something that has little-to-no direct relation to the pragmatic concerns of our life. For ninety minutes or so, cinema creates an opening in life and gives us a chance to fabulate a detour, to meander along life's indirect ways. And yet we often prefer a more "coherent" film that goes straight to the end, that tells us a well-made story. But even under these conditions, there "is always a moment when the cinema meets the unforeseeable or the improvisation, the irreducibility of a present living under the present of narration, and the camera cannot even begin its work without engendering its own improvisations, both as obstacles and as indispensable means" (Deleuze 1986b: 206). Apichatpong's cinema gives us just such moments, which are both a challenge and a condition for his style. In *Mysterious Object at Noon*, the indispensable obstacle is the story of Dogfahr and the boy, which loosely connects the different acts of fabulation and creates openings for each narrator to improvise with the camera but also lays down a challenge for the story editor. How will he illustrate the doubling of Dogfahr? How will he show us the alien boy's transformation into a giant? And Apichatpong's illustration is as heterogeneous as the story itself: it is spoken, written, sung, signed, and acted out (each character by several different actors). Coherence is less important here than *consistency*, the holding together of heterogeneous elements within an assemblage. This question of consistency is crucial for thinking with Apichatpong because his films are often incoherent. Much has been said about how his films – most of them segmented into two or three parts – actually *hold together*. It is often done through a doubling that is felt as an affective intensification (certainly the case in *Tropical Malady*, see Chapter 4). In *Mysterious Object at Noon*, the procedure of the exquisite corpse functions as an enabling constraint ("indispensable obstacle") because it constitutes a shared concern, a concern that holds the film together across its scattered spatial and temporal coordinates. Furthermore, it must be said, the narrator's inventions, haphazard and surprising though they may be, are hardly unheard of. The doublings, transformation, and "devourings" are in fact fairy tale clichés. They are the refrains of popular storytelling and reach into an impersonal past that binds a community even as the cliché disrupts all narrative progression. This is what Gilles Deleuze calls film as "the stroll, the voyage and the continual return journey":

> It happens in any-space-whatever [...] in opposition
> to action which most often unfolded in the
> qualified space-time of the old realism. [...] Now,
> what consolidates all this, are the current clichés
> of an epoch or a moment, sound and visual
> slogans. (1986: 208)

In light of this, one can say that Apichatpong has in fact developed a set of audiovisual slogans by which one can stroll through the entire body of his work. He produces "floating images" that "maintain a set [*ensemble*] in a world without totality" or coherence (Deleuze 1986b: 208). Besides the segmentation of most of his films into several parts (mostly two), think of the many long takes shot from inside a car going down a country road or driving through a city landscape. This cliché allows you to stroll from *Mysterious Object at Noon* to *Uncle Boonmee* via *Blissfully Yours* and, with slight variations, *Tropical Malady*.

Or consider all the scenes in a doctor's office, which link *Mysterious Object* to *Syndromes and a Century* and again *Blissfully Yours* (Fig. 4 and 5). The work of this cliché across Apichatpong's films is to articulate *encounters*: of an individual and an institution (Orn's struggle to obtain medication for the illegal immigrant Min); of modern and traditional medicine (the Monk's herbal potion in *Syndromes*); between physical and spiritual cures

Fig. 4: Still from *Mysterious Object at Noon*, 16 mm (blown up to 35 mm).

Fig. 5: Still from *Blissfully Yours*.

(Dogfahr's amulet). Think also of Boonmee being attended to by the ghost of his wife Huay. The return of these scenes acts as a refrain that reminds us of the multiplicity of experience in Apichatpong's films. Each time we see a doctor argue with her patient about, say, the efficicacy of a homemade remedy, we feel this encounter between different spheres of life all the more intensely because the foregone iterations of the refrain vaguely return to imbue the actual image with the tone of memory and open it towards the future. The cliché, understood as a ready-made phrase if we follow its original meaning in relation to typesetting, is deflected from dead repetition through its activation as a refrain. This refrain has the duplicitous force to hold a film together and at the same time create a rift in the image that opens it to its predecessors but also to an indeterminate to-come.

I pose the problem of consistency in this way to frame my discussion of *The Adventure of Iron Pussy.* Given Apichatpong's recognizable aesthetics, how can one account for a film that clearly diverges from his signature style? Do we have to consider the film an "inconsistency" within the director's "oeuvre"? James Quandt seems to suggest just that:

> Made as a lark on hiatus from *Tropical Malady,*
> *Iron Pussy* was cooked up and co-directed by gay
> performance artist Michael Shaowanasai, and,
> though Joe [i.e. Apichatpong] seems very fond of it,
> it is Shaowanasai's show, despite the many auteurist
> imprints an over-zealous critic can detect. (2009: 58)

Quandt goes to some rhetoric lengths here to all but exclude *The Adventure of Iron Pussy* from Apichatpong's "oeuvre". Moreover, he deplores the filmmaker's various collaborative endeavors: "Alas, Joe prizes collaboration but sometimes gets lost in the process" (Quandt 2009: 60). This is the underlying tone of Quandt's piece on "*The Adventure of Iron Pussy* and Other Collaborations": he assumes a self-contained artistic individuality for a filmmaker who is, in fact, rarely credited as "director" and whose films consistently articulate a plurality of modes of existence and the leakiness of the individual. Perhaps, then, it is through *Iron Pussy* as the odd one out that we can perceive how Apichatpong's films hold together: "Even in a territorial assemblage, it may be the most deterritorialized component, the deterritorializing vector, in other words, the refrain, that assures the consistency of the territory" (Deleuze and Guattari 1987: 327).

The Adventure of Iron Pussy: A Time Machine

Iron Pussy is one of Thai performance artist Michael Shaowanasai's various avatars: a former go-go-boy who finds his vocation as a transvestite secret agent fighting against international crime and for the rights of the downtrodden. Pussy's style and demeanour are inspired by 1960s and '70s Thai movie legend Petchara Chaowarat. The movie itself is a remix of uncountable film clichés, ranging from obsolete genre norms to stereotypical characters, from over-the-top musical scenes to a cliché ending (including a cliffhanger and a Pietà).

> The concept was to simulate the working style of the old Thai films of the past. The film is made as if composed of the junk left in the trash bins of the abandoned Thai film studios. It is designed to celebrate the old style of 'quickie' cinema that nobody makes anymore in contemporary Thai cinema. Among the artifacts used were the lost sounds, the dubbed voices that are so distant but so cherished in memory. (Apichatpong in Quandt 2009: 223)

The Adventure of Iron Pussy is not a parody, nor a caricature. It is a "celebration", a homage to a past that, in its very obsolescence, remains touching. How do we have to think the notion of *simulation* and *composition* here? What does it mean to simulate a working style or to as-if-compose a film?

Cinema always composes with clichés, today perhaps more than ever. Watch any superhero film or romantic comedy and you can easily spot them. But the clichés *of the present* easily go unnoticed; they circulate surreptitiously because they do their job as a narrative device so well. We might not even know our own clichés of the present yet (Sontag 1999: 60). In the case of *Iron Pussy*, however, composition in the mode of the *as-if* is a return to the clichés *of the past*: they can be reanimated but will inevitably bear the ambiguous mark of the ghostly. On the one hand, they are impotent in that they no longer give to see the world as they did in their own time: as serious, suspenseful, action-laden. On the other, and just like ghosts, these clichés *act* in the present by virtue of their quasi-presence: they open perception to that which lies beyond the currently given and beyond the accepted ways of showing the world in cinema. The past returns as potential. Consequently, the notion of simulation does not in this case indicate a false reality. When Apichatpong and Shaowanasai "simulate the working style of the old Thai films of the past", they immediately create a real difference within their lived experience as filmmakers. In this sense, Apichatpong's simulation is not false; rather, it harnesses the powers of the false as it "replaces and supersedes the form of the true, because it poses the simultaneity of incompossible presents" (Deleuze 1989: 131). *Iron Pussy* is an opportunity for Apichatpong to inflect his mode of living with film. How else can we make a film? What are the affordances of "quickie cinema" that other modes of filmmaking lack? As-if-composition is to *Iron Pussy* what the exquisite corpse is to *Mysterious Object*: the enabling constraint that allows for a rigorously vague film procedure. They are two manifestations of the speculative *what-if* mentioned at the beginning of this chapter.

In *Iron Pussy*, this procedure consists in a falsification of our tried-and-tested protocols of composition through an experimentation with the worn-out, with that which can only return by differing with itself. The difference that is produced in the simulation of an obsolete working style is the rediscovery of the joy of filmmaking itself. *Iron Pussy* is not a film that wants to tell a good story; it revels in making images. And nothing makes us feel that joy in cinema like a film cliché that shamelessly exposes itself. Pussy is a trained secret agent: she knows how to do reconnaissance

Fig. 6: Still from *The Adventure of Iron Pussy*.

Fig. 7: Still from *The Adventure of Iron Pussy*.

work and stealthily gather information over her shoulder (Fig. 6); we see her climbing up the wall of a house and immediately know that the scene was shot horizontally on a fake wall (Fig. 7). These shots are all the more delightful because the story doesn't make any sense. Pussy has a number of impossible costume changes (from one shot to the next within the same scene). On a hunting excursion in the jungle, she saves her love interest Tang from a Tiger (!), then confronts him at gunpoint about his drug trafficking, only to learn that the two are in fact brother and sister. At another moment, Tang uses another spy-film cliché as he pulls off the maid-supervisor's face to unmask Major Rungranee from the Special Forces Unit who is also his betrothed. Betrayal? Yes. And Doublings? Yes! And Tiger attacks? Of course! Much as *Mysterious Object*, *Iron Pussy* veers from one stereotype to another, affirming its vitality in each of them.

How are these feelings of vitality and joy created? It is here that *Iron Pussy* and *Mysterious Object* diverge and develop their own procedures. Both films employ clichés as landing sites but in slightly different ways. In *Mysterious Object at Noon*, the cliché provides a safe landing for a story that is precariously suspended between narrators. The cliché allows for a gesture of care, in which each narrator can acknowledge the *act* of fabulation and the collective of storytellers at the same time. It provides a secure discharge for suspense and a familiar point from which to continue. The cliché is a moment of contraction, a flash of the familiar and settled that lays the ground for a fragile novelty. In this sense, the cliché in *Mysterious Object at Noon* is a relay technique that allows for a story to safely circulate within a collective. In *Iron Pussy*, the work of the cliché is not so much to create a storytelling relay but to open onto the history of filmmaking as a practice. We may never believe in the adventure of Iron Pussy, but *The Adventure of Iron Pussy* makes us believe in cinema as a mode of living.[2] Each topos of the spy film genre contributes to this opening onto the past: a poorly executed cut that turns a feeble arm twist into an impressive wrestling throw releases countless memories of stylized editing techniques that have always been too good to be true. Every fake glass bottle that goes down on someone's head shatters into myriad splinters of amusing pasts in which a body could be either knocked out by one bottle or survive a dozen gunshot wounds. Each familiar shot, cut or gesture continues a holding-open of a cinematic past. In *The Adventure of Iron Pussy*, film history provides a liveable milieu for the present.

The sound of the film is central to sustaining this milieu. It must be noted that, contrary to the fullness of ambient sound in most of Apichatpong's films, the soundscape in *Iron Pussy* is flat and artificial. All the voices are dubbed in post-production; each fist punch comes with the same sound effect; the music is right out of the cheapest synthesizer you can imagine. The film wants its viewer to notice the abyss between the image and the sound. It is through this odd discrepancy that we realize that this kind of film is actually a twofold endeavour. And all of a sudden the apparent joy that Shaowanasai takes in posing as Iron Pussy is doubled by the banter of the sound artists. While you may never hear an authentic sound in the film, you can sense a genuine delight in the over-the-top voice acting. When Iron Pussy performs a solitary puja by the river, she is interrupted by a Buddhist nun: the voice actor's surprised "huh" in her voice is mischievously theatrical, inventing a reaction that can hardly be found in Shaowanasai's acting. This kind of dubbing, a relic of the past, is itself an act of fabulation. It complicates and thickens the ecology of the film and effectively invents what the film will be. In the multiplicity of the creative process, the filmmakers craft an aesthetic that is immediately political.

The Politicality of Joy

The aesthetics of the 1970s action film are immediately political because they make us perceive certain concerns of the present differently. Through *Iron Pussy*'s audiovisuals from the past, we get a new perspective on gender normativity and sexuality. In fact, the two often intersect in Thai culture: "There's only one word that means both 'transvestite' and 'gay' in Thai" (Apichatpong in Quandt 2009: 58). How, then, does *Iron Pussy* make us perceive this complex of issues differently? To conclude, I want to suggest that the film modulates perceptions of gender and sexuality through humor and joy.

Resisting a didactic approach, *Iron Pussy* never asserts a strict distinction between gender and sexuality as a corrective to the linguistic and cultural conflation of terms in Thai. It harnesses the confusion as a complexity to create openings for new individuations. Thus, instead of separating out different categories for identification, the film foregrounds the processual dimension of the individual. Against a stabilization of identity (which has found its political expression in identity politics), *Iron Pussy* shows that self-differentiation is in fact a continuous queering. Furthermore, the film shows that thinking and perceiving beyond stable identities needn't be a loss of certainty and agency. The individuations of the film are always joyful creations that affirm experimentation and potential through the body's becoming. Once again, this is shown particularly well in the ambiguous embodiment of Iron Pussy herself: the male body in drag and its female voice remain amusingly disjunct throughout the film. Even though we can easily think them as one character, there is something that persistently exceeds this rational consolidation. I believe that the ethico-aesthetic consistency of Iron Pussy lies here, in a relation between components – male body, female voice – that refuse to connect without "com[ing] into effect in excess over themselves" (Massumi 2011: 20). This excess is the comedic effect, the joyful vibration that the body can't shake off all through the film. *Iron Pussy*'s political acumen lies in this interstice between established modes of identification, in a "relation-of-nonrelation" that is viscerally felt (Massumi 2011: 20). This is not to say that *Iron Pussy* "does not work". On the contrary, the film *works with* the divergent image and sound to create a joyful appreciation of sexual and gender indeterminacy. In this way, *The Adventure of Iron Pussy* harnesses obsolete aesthetic standards to playfully generate new and increasingly complex individuations.

There is a politicality to this playfulness and this joy because they bypass intellectual discourses on gender and sexuality. Before you can resort to received notions of masculinity and femininity, you are already smiling, caught up in the fabulation of Iron Pussy. The beautiful feat of this film consists in making its viewers unwittingly rethink the potentials of a body *through* their very own bodies. Joyfully moving with the image in your seat, you may raise a mischievous eyebrow or purse your sassy lips; you may jerk your head with each blow of Pussy's iron fists as they come down on her enemies with a musical *kapow*! Particles of Pussy's unidentified sex shoot off the screen and prick your body into the uncountable alternatives to established gender identities. In the encounter, you rediscover your body's capacity to engender "a thousand sexes", thousands of sexes (Deleuze and Guattari 1987: 278).[3] This engendering is an open-ended process, in excess of what you understand yourself to be. There is always another sex to be invented, always a +1. Sexuality vivaciously outruns conscious identifications.

In this way, Iron Pussy draws our attention to the futurity that animates drag performances in the present. In resonance with Deleuze's concept of fabulation, Judith Butler describes drag performances as creating "culturally unintelligible" genders belonging to "a set of parodic practices based in performative theory of speech acts that *disrupt* the categories of body, sex, gender, and sexuality" (2006: 186–93, xxxiv, emphasis added). Because this work focuses on the ways in which drag and other parodic practices interfere with established and culturally intelligible conceptions of gender, their main achievement is thought to consist in disrupting those gender conceptions. From this perspective, Iron Pussy challenges our *understanding* of gender as we know it. *Yes*, and more. From the point of view proposed here, one that engages with the immediate experience of an image, it becomes clear that *new genders are already lived before we can even begin to think of them as unintelligible*. For Iron Pussy, gender is not primarily an epistemological problem but one of *vitality*. Before asking "what will and will not constitute an intelligible life" (Butler 2006: xxiii), Pussy raises the question: how do you compose your next gender, collectively? This is also why it is so important to think the mismatched image and sound that compose Pussy's body as *disjunctive* rather than disruptive: the disjunctive synthesis of image and sound is *creative* of a new sex, immediately lived with the image. The cut creates life before it disrupts knowledge.

What, then, if we began to think, feel and live sexuality from the exuberance of the +1? We would be able to recognize the minor differences in sexuality between people who previously occupied the same gender category, between this straight woman and that straight woman, between one transgender person and another. We could perceive convergences and divergences across the entire field of sexualities that have little to do with gender identities. We could resist gender normativity not through opposition but by shooting our innumerable minor differences through molar gender formations. Adventurers like Iron Pussy "produce *n* molecular sexes on the line of flight in relation to the dualism machines they cross right through" (Deleuze and Guattari 1987: 277).

What if... *The Adventures of Iron Pussy* foregrounds speculative joy to explore how gender and sexuality can be *lived* differently. *Mysterious Object at Noon* embraces speculation to ground a community not in a discourse of national identity but in the care for a collectively told story. These films continue their speculative work after the last image has left the screen: within the viewer, as a feeling of vitality, life's enjoyment of itself. To feel the films of Apichatpong is to infuse life with the zest of fabulation.

Notes

1. The expression "life-living" is used by Erin Manning in *Always More Than One* to articulate the life's propensity towards collective individuation (2013: 60, passim). As such, life-living is closely related to Gilles Deleuze's notion of "a life" with, however, an added emphasis on the creative movement of vitality (Deleuze 2006: 384-389).

2. Thomas Elsaesser and Malte Hagener propose that cinema should be thought of as a "life form" (2010: 10). The question arises then of *how we live with* different cinemas. How do or can we live with the films of Apichatpong as opposed to rom-coms and superhero movies?

3. The notion of "engendering" is adopted from Manning (2007: 84–109).

Works Cited

Butler, Judith. *Gender Trouble: Feminism and the Subversion of Identity.* New York: Routledge, 2006.

Deleuze, Gilles. *Nietzsche and Philosophy.* London: Continuum, 1986a.

Deleuze, Gilles. *Cinema 1: The Movement-Image.* Minneapolis: University of Minnesota Press, 1986b.

Deleuze, Gilles. *Cinema 2: The Time-Image.* Minneapolis: University of Minnesota Press, 1989.

Deleuze, Gilles. *Two Regimes of Madness: Texts and Interviews 1975–1995.* Ed. David Lapoujade. Los Angeles/Cambridge: Semiotext(e)/MIT Press, 2006.

Deleuze, Gilles, and Félix Guattari. *A Thousand Plateaus. Capitalism and Schizophrenia, vol. 2.* Trans. Brian Massumi. Minneapolis: University of Minnesota Press, 1987.

Elsaesser, Thomas, and Malte Hagener. *Film Theory: An Introduction Through the Senses.* New York: Routledge, 2010.

Manning, Erin. *Politics of Touch: Sense, Movement, Sovereignty.* Minneapolis: University of Minnesota Press, 2007.

Manning, Erin. *Always More Than One: Individuation's Dance.* Durham: Duke University Press, 2013.

Massumi, Brian. *Semblance and Event: Activist Philosophy and the Occurrent Arts.* Cambridge: The MIT Press, 2011.

Nietzsche, Friedrich. *Thus Spoke Zarathustra: A Book for All and None.* Trans. Walter Kaufmann. London: Penguin, 1975.

Quandt, James. *"The Adventure of Iron Pussy* and Other Collaborations".
Apichatpong Weerasethakul. Ed. James Quandt. Wien: Synema,
2009. 58–62.

Sontag, Susan. "Notes on 'Camp.'" *Camp: Queer Aesthetics and the Per-
forming Subject.* Ed. Fabio Cleto. Ann Arbor: University of Michigan
Press, 1999. 53–65.

One of the reasons why Guattari's thinking lends itself so well to analyzing the aesthetic challenges presented by Apichatpong's cinema is because his schizoanalytic cartography of ontological functors machines the production of subjectivity. If by "ontology" we take Guattari at his word and insist on it being traversed by the four ontological functors, then the term implies a hauntology: it is always haunted by the "what if?" of functors having functioned differently, which haunt every movement, every machination, every bifurcation, every line of flight. The singularity of (Thai) history is haunted by the multiplicity from which its own becoming emerges. Making felt, and sometimes even making seen, the multiplicities that never actualized are key to the Weerasethakul-operation and what makes him an archivist of abandoned potential, of the virtualities that history failed to select in its process of actualization.

Machines don't distinguish between the living and the dead: either can be put into motion and made to function. Either can desire. Deleuze and Guattari's rereading of the Freudian theorizations of Eros and Thanatos applies here:

> [I]t is absurd to speak of a death desire that would presumably be in qualitative opposition to the life desires. Death is not desired, there is only death that desires, by virtue of the body without organs or the immobile motor, and there is also life that desires, by virtue of the working organs. There we do not have two desires but two parts, two kinds of desiring-machine parts, in the dispersion of the machine itself.[1]

Life and death: two regimes of machinic desire. Once the notion of being is approached from the perspective of machinic multiplicities, ontology – and even hauntology – takes on an entirely different sense.

Whether hauntology or machinic ontology, both insist on the reality of the virtual. Hence the importance of registering the presence of non-presence in Derrida's hauntology and the significance of the nth term in Guattari's schizoanalysis. The virtual is a quantum of alterity. That's exactly why we turn to the schizoanalytic cartographies, because by deploying quadrants, and insisting on a fourth term in analysis, a cartography is opened up onto alterity. The fourth term is the nth term. Something – even something spectral, a virtual non-thing – can always enter the event, and in relational movement, recompose its ontological organization.

By thinking the event of the production of human existence as a truly machinic process, any natural distinction between the living and the dead starts to dissolve. The living can haunt the dead as much as the dead can haunt the living. Are not events always "haunted" by the n factor of being's *more-than*?

Is the word "ontology" still appropriate under these conditions of machinic ontogenesis? We think it can remain a useful, and vital, frame of analysis, as long as the novelty of machinic processes is emphasized every step of the way, so as to encourage belief in the potential of subjective recomposition based on encounters with alterity.

By privileging the machinic co-composition of the living and the dead in the realization of the cinematic-image-as-event, the relationship between the felt and the seen takes on a new complexity. Because forces need not be seen to be made felt – they need not even be "alive" in the organic sense of the term. Apichatpong's ghosts are felt, and this shifts the ontological composition of the scene of their (non)presence. In some instances, they are also rendered visible, and given corporeal form. To a certain degree, that's why Apichatpong's images are "ecosophically sensitive" – they adopt a range of perceptibility that accommodates difference, and different degrees of visibility. But the being made visible of the ghosts which populate Apichatpong's world is not entirely congruent with their being made felt. There are indefinite animals, ghosts, and spirits who are felt throughout the film world – even if they never actually, visually appear. Once you are absorbed in Apichatpong's film world, it is impossible not to feel them all around!

That which is made seen is only ever the cusp of all that is felt. Not that the seen represents, or stands in for all that is felt. But rather it carries the affective charge of all of the multiple and virtual intensities that traverse and intersect it. Watching Apichatpong's films, we know there are other monkey-ghosts populating the jungle, because we can feel them even if we can never see them. This phenomenon can be taken as a cinematic variant of what Deleuze and Guattari write in *Anti-Oedipus*: that we never make love with each other, we make love to worlds.[2] So when the spectral is given visibility, it makes an entire range of spectrality felt along with it, even if it remains hidden by opacity. Boonsong isn't an individual monkey-ghost, he is the enunciatory limit of an endangered, or even extinct, species – an entire world of collective spectrality that is inseperable from his very existence and that his being seen makes felt in a myriad of ways (découpage, long takes, etc.): a true haunting of his being by the excess of the world that machinically produces it.

Ghosts don't need to be made seen in order for the image to have enough contact with the radical alterity of the outside (including the force of "other" temporalities/histories) to prove themselves amenable to recomposition. It's precisely this metastability, this openness to the outside implicit in actual formations, which politicizes Apichatpong's work since it truly believes that the world is up for grabs, and that interventions (whether they be filmic or meditative) make a real difference. Peace is at once a pragmatics of belief and commitment: a belief in the potential for subjective recomposition (a broadening of feeling) and a commitment to remaining open to an encounter with alterity that could bring it about.

Notes

1. Deleuze, Gilles and Félix Guattari. *Anti-Oedipus: Capitalism and Schizophrenia*, vol. 1. Trans. Robert Hurley, Mark Seem and Helen R. Lane. Minneapolis: University of Minnesota Press, 1983. 329.

2. Ibid. 294.

Adam Szymanski

Uncle Boonmee Who Can Recall His Past Lives and the Ecosophic Aesthetics of Peace

The fantastical population of Apichatpong's film worlds – the mystical creatures, benevolent ghosts and talking animals who repeatedly appear and disappear in their travelling of time – offer an oblique access point into Thailand's war-torn history, especially the American-backed military occupation and communist purging of Isaan province that took place from the 1960s through to the 1980s. As a child, Apichatpong became intimately familiar with the region and its history after his parents relocated their medical practices to the province out of solidarity with its leftist organizing. He witnessed that amidst the violence of the occupation, villagers threatened by the military fled their homes and hid in the jungle.[1] Many of them never returned. *Uncle Boonmee Who Can Recall His Past Lives* is set in Isaan,[2] and is premised on the affective-historical fact that the region's purging is still felt by the widows and descendants of the disappeared communists, despite the reigning royalist regime's attempts to silence and censor this history in the name of national unity.[3]

Isaan is thus a site of conflicted signification in Thai culture. As a principally rural and agricultural province it lends itself to signifying as "rural utopia" and "cornerstone of Thai heritage", two ideological discourses taken up by forces as opposed as left-wing intellectuals and royalist-nationalists (Boehler 2011: 293). In defiance of these national heritage discourses, the rural space of the Isaan jungle simultaneously signifies as anti-nation[4] because of the region's historical association with communist resistance (and its ties to various ethnic minorities in Thailand such as the Chinese and Laotians).[5] *Uncle Boonmee* does more than signify on one side of this ideological conflict between nation and anti-nation, geopolitical centre and margin, royalist and communist. In defiance of censorship threats and distribution difficulties in Thailand, Apichatpong's cinema endeavours to bring back the disappeared peoples who were driven into the jungle and lost to military aggression and to make reverberate the ethos that the government tried to extinguish when it disappeared the people of Isaan. From the heart of the jungle – a blot on the Thai political unconscious – *Uncle Boonmee* recomposes the thresholds of the three ecologies, and in doing so, brings repressed cultural memories out of obscurity to bear on a society that has had great difficulty acknowledging the willed omissions of its history, including the peoples and values that have been lost.

Ecosophy as a Call for Peace

Human subjectivity, the socius and the environment together constitute what Félix Guattari calls "the three ecologies". The practice of ethically-politically thinking the pragmatics of their co-composition is called "ecosophy", and its chief problematic "is that of the production of human existence itself in new historic contexts" (Guattari 2008: 24). It is possible to read Guattari's late works on ecosophy as a call for "peace", at least in the sense that A.N. Whitehead gives to the word. As process theologist Mary Elizabeth Mullino Moore points out, Whiteheadian peace "is not the absence of war and violence, but the presence of other relationships ([in Whitehead's words,] 'a broadening of feeling') with the wider world" (Mullino Moore 2006: 205). Finding more heteropoetic ways of living with the "other" in "other relationships" is central to the ethico-political task of ecosophy, and its therapeutic investment in the production of subjectivity. *The Three Ecologies* concludes with an appeal for a revitalized relationship to alterity, "new social and aesthetic practices, new practices of the Self in relation to the other, to the foreign, the strange [...] new solidarities, a new gentleness [...] Individuals must become both more united and increasingly different" (Guattari 2008: 45, 51). With a similar concern for the value of alterity, Isabelle Stengers builds on Guattari's ecosophy to define "peace as the ecological production of actual togetherness where 'ecological' means the aim is not toward a unity beyond differences, which would reduce those differences through a goodwill reference to abstract principles of togetherness, but toward the creation of concrete, interlocked, asymmetrical, and always partial graspings" (Stengers 2002: 248–9). To compose peace is to compose togetherness-in-difference, to assemble a collective that holds, not in spite, but because of its differences in a way that broadens the affective range of collective experience.

Encounters with alterity are opportunities for surpassing established subject positions. The adventurous character of peace – its broadening of feeling – comes about through this encounter with alterity, where self and other cease to be what they were by bringing a novel event of relation into existence. Whitehead writes:

> Peace is a broadening of feeling due to the emergence of some deep metaphysical insight, unverbalized and yet momentous in its coordination of values. Its first removal is the stress of acquisitive feeling arising from the soul's preoccupation with itself. Peace carries with it a surpassing of personality. [...] Peace is the removal of inhibition and not its introduction. It results in a wider sweep of conscious interest. It enlarges the field of attention. Thus Peace is self-control at its

widest, – at the width where the 'self' has been lost, and interest has been transferred to coordinations wider than personality. [...] Peace is the barrier against narrowness. (Whitehead 1967: 285)

By broadening feeling and widening consciousness to encompass the play of differences that engender an ecology, peace re-coordinates the values governing the production of subjectivity, resulting in a jouissance of collective reindividuation that recasts the world's quantum of potential for cohabitation.

Two scenes in *Uncle Boonmee* are particularly illustrative of how Apichatpong uses ecosophic aesthetics to visualize the processual emergence of such a peace. The first alters its range of perceptibility – and feeling – in order to visualize various degrees of alterity under one ecologically sensitive image. It clears the way for one of the film's concluding scenes, which finally accomplishes the implementation of peace and the overcoming of reified personality through the aesthetic creation of an event that shocks the coordinates of selfhood; coordinates that had started to loosen as soon this alterious collective from the first scene came into existence. Apichatpong's aesthetic composition with the imperceptible makes return a repressed ethico-political force that reconditions the ontological functors immanent to the three ecologies in the service of actualizing a novel sense of peace.[6]

Encountering Alterity, Broadening Feeling

The first exemplary scene depicts the film's protagonist, Uncle Boonmee (Thanapat Saisaymar), an ill plantation owner, his sister-in-law Jen (Jenjira Pongpas), and his nephew Tong (Sakda Kaewbuadee) calmly eating dinner inside of a windowless veranda. Then, out of nowhere, a ghost materializes. It turns out to be Huay (Natthakarn Aphaiwonk), Boonmee's deceased wife. Overcoming their initial surprise, the three characters speak with her about Boonmee's illness and impending death, until they are joined by an even more surprising guest. This time it's (what the subtitles refer to as) a "monkey-ghost" with bright red eyes, covered head-to-toe in thick black hair. The monkey-ghost claims to be Boonsong (Geerasak Kulhong), Boonmee and Huay's long-lost son who went missing after taking a trip into the jungle many years ago.

This scene, like the entire film, is entirely devoid of point of view shots. In their absence, the various depersonalized forces active within the ecology of the film world come to guide the logic of the relationship between shots, constituting an ecosophic découpage (and corresponding editing structure).[7] There is action to propel the scene's formal organization, yet this action is as driven by memories, ghosts, far-off sounds and animals as it is by any human-centered drama. The logic of Apichatpong's cut is irrational from the point of view of the human subject and can only be accounted for through a consideration of the unknown and the unseen that are made felt in the broader ecology. The scene's découpage spatially situates the different characters within their broader environment and temporally situates them with regards to their past transformations. It opens with a long shot of a veranda, as seen from the surrounding jungle (Fig. 8). The interior space marks the only source of light amidst the long shot of the dark rural area. The characters' voices are heard in the distance. Cut to inside the veranda, the cinematography squarely lines up within its box-shaped architectural form (Fig. 9). The camera moves in closer to compose medium shots of the three characters sitting at a table (Fig. 10, 11, 12 and 13). Then the film mounts a dark landscape shot with the veranda now completely out of frame, decentered in an unknown direction (Fig. 14). The sound of an approaching storm rumbles across the soundtrack before the film cuts to an adjacent shot of bushes swaying and rustling. "What's that sound?" one of the characters asks, before a cut back inside, to the original medium shot of the table (Fig. 15). The subsequent few shots show Boonsong's

Fig. 8

Fig. 9

Fig. 10

Fig. 11

Fig. 12

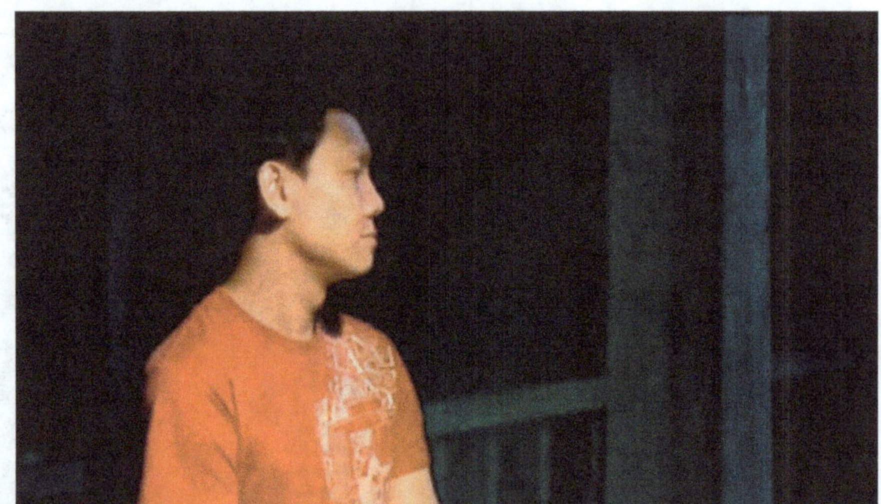

Fig. 13

Fig. 14

Fig. 15

Fig. 16

entrance. On the axis of spatiality, the cutaway shots of the mountain, bushes, and neon bug-zappers break from human-centered schemas of scopic organization that coordinate the ecology according to an anthropocentric hierarchy of value. The localized, character-driven action is fragmented and repositioned by the active presence of the adjacent environment just outside the veranda.

The scene also intensively channels Boonsong's mental interiority, his recollection of the events that have brought him to where he is today and made him what he has become. When he recounts the story of his past transformations, the camera takes on a new fluidity, which is abruptly juxtaposed with the scene's darkness and rigidity (Fig. 16). Through a découpage equally sensitive to material and mental intensity, the past is made an ecological force. The film sees beyond the actuality of any given plane of temporality and instead renders visible their mutual co-composition of the film world. The present is coloured with a splash of pastness, as Boonsong's recollection interjects into the dinner table gathering and its environmental surround. In beginning to recount his story, Boonsong says, "There are many beings outside right now… spirits and hungry animals, like me." As a sensitive character in an equally sensitive film ecology, he can feel them, even if he can't see them. Boonsong's story recalls how he transformed from an ordinary human photographer to a red-eyed monkey-ghost after he became obsessed with finding the strange creature that had once appeared in the background of one of his landscape photographs. The images of the past that accompany Boonsong's recollection appear as a shared collective heritage. There are no clichéd wipes or dissolves, only an abrupt cut from a shot behind the back of Jen's head to Boonsong's human form inside of a dark room for photography development (Fig. 17). The cut is prompted by his narration of the story, words that all of the characters hear. These images are not psychologized, residing inside of Boonsong's head. These images, as much as they make up Boonsong's experience and memory,

Fig. 17

Fig. 18

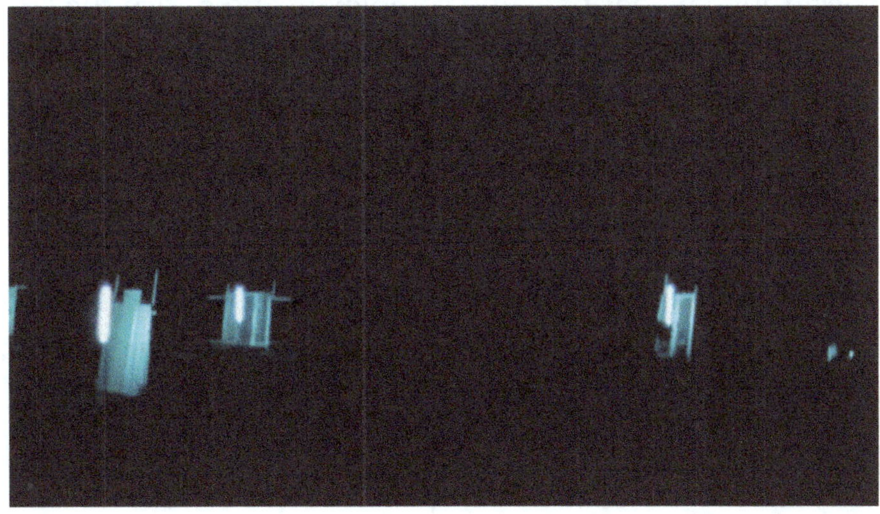

Fig. 19

are exteriorized and socialized – made a concrete part of the shared ecology (to the extent that they can even be affected by others in the scene). At one point in the recollection, Jen says "excuse me" and gets up from the table to go sit on a nearby bench. The recollection immediately stops and cuts back to the present (Fig. 18 and 19). All of the characters at the table have access to the recollection and the ability to stop it, because the recollection doesn't belong solely to Boonsong, entrenched in an inaccessible past. It belongs to their shared ecology. Memories affect others, and in Apichatpong's ecosophical aesthetics, others can affect memories.

The ecosophic logic of the découpage described above diverges from *découpage en plan américain* (also called classical découpage); the logic of the relationship between shots that governs most classical Hollywood cinema.[8] Under the classical system, character-driven shot sequences advance a narrative that reproduces visual codes predicated on stock character behaviour, gaze, and movement. This shooting style is most often contrasted with *découpage en profondeur* (shooting in depth). In découpage en profondeur each plane of depth within the shot is in equally sharp focus and part of what excited André Bazin about this artistic development was its ability to "embrace the totality of the event" (Bazin 1997: 103, translation modified). In the oft-cited Wellesian vein of découpage en profondeur, background planes of action complexify and enrich the story and allow for an expanded number of associations between elements in a single shot to be drawn by the spectator, all without recourse to montage. *Uncle Boonmee* is exemplary of découpage en profondeur, but with a key exception: it has no background to be in or out of focus. It has an "outside", a blacked-out zone of metamorphosis[9] without concrete form that puts the foreground of character drama into contact with the indetermination of pure opacity.[10] Ghosts (who used to be human) emerge from this zone of opacity where the jungle lies, and they come out into the light. They are made visible and their memories are depersonalized and made equally accessible to all, provoking a shift in the scene's ontological consistency.

Guattari's *Schizoanalytic Cartographies* advances the theory that each assemblage of enunciation, or event, is composed of four ontological functors that together give the assemblage its ontological consistency. These functors include existential Territories (T), Fluxes of materiality (F), machinic Phyla of diagrammatic organization (Θ) and incorporeal Universes of value (U). In a passage from *Guattari's Diagrammatic Thought* worth quoting at length, Janell Watson provides a very clear and useful summary of the functors that undergird the myriad cartographies of Guattari's schizoanalytic thought experiments:

> *Fluxes* include physical matter and physical signals; these are subject to the coordinates of energetic quanta, space, and time. The abstract machinic *Phyla* comprise evolution; Guattari's deterritorializing abstract machines; and blueprints, plans, diagrams, rules and regulation (in the cybernetic sense of control mechanisms). Existential *Territories* include subjective identity, the sense of self, and existential 'apprehension.' The incorporeal *Universes* of reference are made up of values, nondiscursive references, and virtual possibility; these 'escape the energetic, legal, evolutionary, and existential coordinates of the three preceding domains.' (Watson 2009: 99)

Cinematographic images, like any other event of perception, are assemblages of enunciation produced through the co-composition of each of the four ontological functors. Firstly, images have a material basis in the Fluxes: signifying and asignifying visual and aural material made up of colours, bodies, movements, landscapes, and text. These cinematic Fluxes function in the realm of sensuous perceptibility. The machinic Phyla can be read as the set of organizing principles at work in an image. Depending on the image, there could be many of these operating at once, in sync or in opposition to one another. Organizing principles can refer to generic and industrial standards, national cinema traditions, and intertextual references, in addition to the social norms and conventions that may be relayed through a film's dissemination. Both Fluxes and Phyla lie on the side of the actual. Incorporeal Universes and existential Territories contribute to the image virtually. The Territories inform how characters within the filmic world are positioned, often through the granting or denying of scopic agency via point-of-view shots. Finally, Universes of value inflect the image's horizon of references and the coordination of value, giving sense to character subjectivities (T), image intensities (F), and the governing structures of the film (Θ). Together, the four ontological functors co-compose the filmic reality.[11]

For the sake of clarity, the ontological functors have been described separately, but they are never in fact separate. An assemblage of enunciation is dynamically composed out of the reality of the relation immanent to its functioning. In Guattari's own words: "They will only be able to sustain their own configurations through the relations that they entertain with each other; they will be required to change state and status as a function of their overall Assemblage" (Guattari 2013: 27). In order live up to its name, a functor must indeed function – it must move. Starting from a movement in any one of these quadrants, an entire ecology can be reworked (for an ecology is fundamentally an assemblage of enunciation). Or rather, an entire ecology can't help but be reworked by one of the functors' very functioning, precisely because the functioning of a functor is simultaneously a relational movement between the four.[12]

Uncle Boonmee's dinner table scene offers an idiosyncratic take on depth of field (nourished by the opacity of the outside) to invite consideration of its ontological depth. From this perspective, whole domains of desire imperceptible on the surface of the image are if not "brought to light" and rendered sensuously perceptible then at least brought nonsensuously to thought, in their opacity. Each of the four ontological functors is active in the cinematographic image, but only the Fluxes are sensuously perceptible. The domain of Fluxes is both actual and real, whereas the machinic Phyla, incorporeal Universes of value and existential Territories are all inflected by either the nonsensuous realms of the possible or the virtual.[13] The aesthetic strategy of this scene makes the ontological depth of Apichatpong's film world felt, without needing to visually represent all that is virtually active yet out of sight.[14] The spontaneous arrival of alterity is certainly registered by the Fluxes, as the image alters its range of perceptibility in order to accommodate the bodies that emerge from the darkness of the jungle. Huay's translucent ghost body is registered right next to Boonsong who is covered in pitch-black fur. This feat in découpage completely alters the semiotic arrangement (F) of the image in a manner that allows for diverse forms of life and modes of existence (ghosts, animals, disappeared peoples) to be convoked by the very same image. If this actual semiotic arrangement is an index of anything, it is an index of the virtual movements of the four ontological functors in the process of recomposition, and not an index of a pre-existing reality (the profilmic). With the collective emergence convoked, the abstract machine (Θ) governing the possibility of the event's actual development is different than it was before. The table that originally arranged the characters around it in the act of eating together has become a locus for the emergence of difference harboured by opacity. The real virtual domain of diegetic subjectivity (T) is also altered by the unlikely appearances of Huay and Boonsong – the group subjectivity shifts in composition, as two *others* fold into the scene. Through this mutual inclusion, notions of family, togetherness, and collectivity take on meanings that extend across species and the divide between life and death. In conjunction with all of this movement, which create a new ontological consistency, Boonmee comes to regret his anti-communist violence and attributes his liver disease to the bad karma of these past actions. The family's relational dynamics are renewed and they take on a new collective character, accommodating alterious forms of life and modes of existence along with memories and premonitions, and whole virtual universes of value that these degrees of difference bring into the scene. The renewal is so profound as to constitute a "group subject", in that it becomes a group "that respects the heterogeneity of its component parts, and does not try to subsume them under an illusion of unity; that it is a group in process that explores and changes as conditions change, instead of hardening into a paralytic hierarchy of mutually exclusive terms with assigned value" (Massumi 1988: 440). Values (U), qualities of virtual possibility, are also modified in the recomposition of group subjectivity, because when Boonsong and Huay emerge from the jungle they carry a repressed set of political values and cultural memories with them. The jungle – a space of hiding, fleeing and taking cover for the communists liquidated by the military invasion of Isaan province – is here a point of emergence. Boonsong and Huay are different when they come out of the jungle, having been transformed by the unrepresentable horrors that took place within it. Emerging and asserting the difference of one's metamorphosis is an unrepresentable historical testimony that demands to be accommodated in the scene of presence. Shifting to accommodate the expressive presence of the repressed is a relational movement of the four ontological functors that alters the assemblage of enunciation, resingularizing the three ecologies. A small group's subjective orientation shifts, making peace with the alterious re-emergence of remnants from an opaque past made virtually active and nonsensuously perceptible. The schizoanalytic cartography demands to be redrawn once more, to account for this broadening of feeling that we could call peace.

Disappearing/Reappearing: Surpassing Personality

Uncle Boonmee and a number of other short films and installations from Apichatpong's *Primitive* project[15] extensively use images of male teenage youth from Nabua, a "town of widows", that suffered immensely at the hands of the military occupation and communist purging.[16] The choice of teenage boys is significant since they are the descendants of the disappeared men and are orphans of the town of widows. Their presence carries the legacy of their disappeared fathers and widowed mothers along with the story of their past struggles for communism. In another important scene that facilitates the implementation of peace, Boonmee has a nightmarish "dream of the future" where "past people are made to disappear". The scene uncannily invokes what Walter Benjamin has to say about the ephemerality of historical images: "Every image of the past that is not recognized by the present as one of its own concerns threatens to disappear irretrievably" (Benjamin 2007: 255). *Uncle Boonmee* shows how Benjamin's observation is true yet incomplete. Yes, the present carries a selective function; selecting presence – or what Whitehead calls the actual occasion[17] – out of the possibilities that a given process has made available to it. Yet what *Uncle Boonmee* adds to this account is that the present not only chooses which images to remember and forget based on its own concerns, but that the presence of an image, or a remembering, can doubly conceal a disappearance, an active forgetting. The forced disappearance of Isaan communists during the Thai military invasion is a prime example. As a people made to disappear, their image is charged with that very disappearance, to the extent that in order to maintain the status quo, such an image must be concealed and censored, even to the point of the image's (and not just the people's) disappearance. The disappearance of the image of Isaan communists in Thailand cannot at all be accounted for based on the fact that the present does not see it as one of its own concerns. Conversely, the very fact of the communists' disappearance, along with the disappearance of their image, can be attributed to them being a pressing concern to the current Thai political context. The present, so concerned that such an image could usher in a new ethico-political consistency that calls for making peace with this lingering past, restricts the conditions for its appearance. Maybe after long enough the present will no longer need to repress this image if the social landscape has changed to such a degree that its reappearance loses the power to shock subjectivity. In any case, Apichatpong's work is a high-stakes wager on the chance that the reappearance of the disappeared, this making active of the past, can prompt ecological recomposition.[18]

Boonmee's "dream of the future" enacts this wager. On the eve of his death, Boonmee, the ghost of his ex-wife Huan, his sister-in-law Jen, and Tong (the same characters from the dinner table scene) make a pilgrimage to an enormous cave where Boonmee enters a divinatory reverie. The dream is conveyed through ten still photographs that disrupt the film's live-action flow. Boonmee's voiceover monologue reads as follows:

> Boonmee: What's wrong with my eyes. They are open but I can't see a thing? Or are my eyes closed?

> Jen: Maybe you need time for your eyes to adjust to the dark.

> Boonmee: This cave is like a womb, isn't it? I was born here in a life I can't recall. I only know that I was born here. I don't know if I was a human or an animal, a woman or a man.

> [Dream sequence of ten still photographs begins]

> Boonmee: Last night, I dreamt of the future. I arrived there in a sort of time machine. The future city was ruled by an authority able to make anybody disappear.

When they found 'past people,' they shone a light at them. That light projected images of them onto the screen. From the past, until the arrival in the future. Once those images appeared, these 'past people' disappeared. I was afraid of being captured by the authorities because I had many friends in this future. I ran away. But wherever I ran, they still found me. They asked me if I knew this road. I told them I didn't know. And then I disappeared.

The monologue is interlaced with ten still photos which can be briefly described as follows:

Photo one: In a straw coloured open field, a person in an ape suit with a rope tied around its neck is led by a young man in paramilitary attire (Fig. 20).

Photo two: A medium close-up shot of three young soldiers laying on the grass. The pattern of the shadows that cover them resemble the pattern of their camouflage uniforms (Fig. 21).

Photo three: An eaten away tree leaf takes on the texture of the camouflage pattern and hangs in-between the faces of three young soldiers and the chest of another (Fig. 22).

Photo four: Again, two soldiers lying on the ground amidst the bushes with the rifles resting beside them. They camouflage into their green and brown surroundings (Fig. 23).

Photo five: A large group of military men dispersed throughout a field similar to the one seen in the first photo. A mysterious orange (human? animal?) figure walks in the background (Fig. 24).

Photo six: Medium straight-on shot of the ape figure roped up by the neck, held by the soldier seen in the first photo. They are still in the same field (Fig. 25).

Photo seven: The same young men, now dressed in civilian attire, throw stones out of frame to the right. Is the ape figure the target (Fig. 26)?

Photo eight: The ape figure with his arms around a group of six armed soldiers, looking directly at the camera as if posing for a group photo (Fig. 27).

Photo nine: Five of the young men take a photo of a shirtless sixth laying out on the ground. Is he dead or alive (Fig. 28)?

Photo ten: Crop circles on a dirt path (Fig. 29).

Fig. 20

Fig. 21

Fig. 22

Fig. 23

Fig. 24

Fig. 25

Fig. 26

Fig. 27

Fig. 28

Fig. 29

The phrasing of Boonmee's voiceover suggests that he is the ape figure – possibly a man inside of an ape suit – who arrives in the future "wearing" a different body. However, this is merely one possible interpretation. He could very well be one of the soldiers, one of the civilians, the group as a whole, or even the photographer of the images. There is a real uncertainty as to where to locate him in his own dream, which fits in completely with the ecosophic logic of the dinner table scene's découpage. Boonmee's dream is not really *his* dream at all. The sunny photographs of the dream rip through the slowly paced and opacity filled images of the present in a manner that parallels

Boonsong's earlier recollection. The dream is not localized within Boonmee's psyche, cordoned off from the world. It surpasses Boonmee's personality, enters into the shared ecology. Boonmee is not even identifiable in "his own" dream; he can barely recognize himself in it. It makes little difference whether Boonmee is in fact the ape, the soldiers, or the photographer taking the pictures of these characters – Boonmee cannot find himself in the future. The impossibility of being identified in a dream of one's "own" future proves unbearable to one's self.

Boonmee sees the future as a time where a pervasive conflict plays out between the people of the future and the people of the past. Even if it remains undetermined exactly where he figures in the dream, or what body he identifies with, he is nevertheless *there*, as are Jen, Tong and Huay. They are enmeshed in a future where they do not have a defined place, and yet they are implicated in its inter-generational and inter-species violence. The prospect of living in a future completely incompatible with one's notion of both "self" and "future" instigates a reappraisal of them both. The future becomes a site in dire need of reconfiguration along the lines of a new ontological consistency of peace, in order to make room for the appearance of the self. Yet the very notion of self will need to become other than it presently is in order to fabricate the future condition for its own habitability. For it is largely humankind's unyielding will to dominate difference that led to the prospect of a future where alterity is suffocated to begin with (in other words, a future not so different from the past). Boonmee and his companions are caught in a double bind: cease to exist or exist amidst the uninhabitable. Making this realization shocks their subjectivity (T). Having shaken the existential territory of the self, the future needs to be re-speculated, accounting for this quality of functional alterity that has rendered the ecology slightly more accommodating and less self-assured.

Now that Boonmee's sense of self has been rattled by the shock of the dream, new possibilities for the organization of ontological consistency have been ushered in. Peace is given a chance. Here, in Apichatpong's cinema, the sons of the "town of widows", marginalized and invisible in the Thai political landscape, claim a presence that defies their historical disappearance. Diegetically, Boonmee is shocked and this visual confrontation forces him to reassess his very sense of self on the eve of his death. He can no longer rationalize and justify the actions of his past (which included purging the communists of Isaan), now that he sees a future in which his fate could be as arduous as theirs. *Uncle Boonmee* has made the absent present and the ontological consistency of the film's images has broadened feeling to accommodate the disappeared, in all of their alterity. Apichatpong uses aesthetic experimentation to more fully perceive the movement of the ecology in order to make peace with those whose existence has been denied, whose way of life has been extinguished and whose values have been denigrated. *Uncle Boonmee* has listened to the disappeared – those who were killed and whose memory has been excluded from official nationalist discourse – and has given them presence by expanding its range of perceptibility. The speculative risk of the film, which brings back the disappeared in defiance of the powers-that-be, is that such a modulation on the plane of the image, a modulation that brings the disappeared to perceptibility and enunciation can, when seeded in the world and into the Thai mediascape, provoke a similar type of modulation. Putting the ontological functors immanent to the film image in touch with the functors of the world in which the film lives and circulates: the force of art in life. As such, *Uncle Boonmee* carries the potential to broaden feeling towards an ethico-political paradigm of peace that surpasses personality yet respects the right to singularity, and thus cares for the alterious contrasts of the world, even the ones which have not yet been made to (re)appear.

Notes

1. For an autobiographical account of Apichatpong's intimate relation-
    ship to the occupation and more anecdotes about the role that the
    jungle plays in Apichatpong's engagement with the Thai political
    unconscious, see "The Memory of Nabua. A Note on the *Primitive
    Project*" (2009a: 192–206).

2. Isaan is still today one of the most economically disadvantaged
    regions of Thailand, making it a bastion of red shirt sympathies with
    an antagonistic relationship to yellow shirt urbanites. In 2005–2006
    the Thai People's Alliance for Democracy or colloquially, the Yellow
    Shirts, organized mass protests against former Prime Minister
    Thaksin Shinawatra resulting in a coup d'état. The pro- and anti-
    Thaksin tensions continue to dominate the Thai political landscape
    with a subsequent political crisis in 2008 and yet another coup
    d'état which deposed Thaksin's younger sister and business mag-
    nate Yingluck Shinawatra in 2014.

3. Censorship is an active challenge to politicized filmmaking in
    Thailand, and Apichatpong Weerasethakul is one of the nation's
    most prominent voices of opposition to the censorship legisla-
    tion in place. The Motion Pictures and Video Act B.E. 2551 (2008)
    recently modified the 1930 Film Act and implemented a new rat-
    ing system, yet it still allows for the state to ban films from being
    shown in the Kingdom if they are deemed by the National Film
    and Video Committee (which includes the nation's chief of police)
    to "undermine social order or moral decency, or that might have
    an impact on the security and pride of the nation" (Rithdee 2007).
    For Apichatpong's critique of the (then proposed) legislation, see
    Weerasethakul (2009b).

4. Philip Rosen (1996) sets up the nation/anti-nation dialectic in order
    to emphasize how there exists an anti-national component that
    always troubles national cinemas.

5. See Casella (1970) for a historical account of how communist
    insurgency in Thailand is tied to the political activities of Chinese
    and Vietnamese minorities based in Khon Kaen (the city where
    Apichatpong would later grow up). Alpern (1975) also outlines the
    ethnic and linguistic makeup of the northeast and its importance to
    the Communist Party of Thailand's guerrilla strategies in the 1950s–
    60s. Thomas (1986) traces the rise and decline of Communist Party
    organization in Thailand from the 1960s through to the 1980s.

6. I use the term "repressed" here because it best articulates the psychic and social character of the targeted militarized purging seen in Isaan province. In Deleuze and Guattari's chapter "Social Repression and Psychic Repression" in *Anti-Oedipus* (1983) they detail how psychic repression and social repression reproduce and reinforce one another, in order to prevent desire's revolutionary force from disrupting established social structures. This psychosocial conception of repression posits that both desiring production and repression are inherently collective acts which condition the life of an ecology and thus overrun the limits of Freud's individualized subject who possess a personalized unconscious of repressed desires. Thus my use of the term repression throughout this paper should not be confused with repression as used in the more limited Freudian sense, wherein repression is "an operation whereby the subject attempts to repel, or to confine to the unconscious, representations (thoughts, images, memories) which are bound to an instinct. Repression occurs when to satisfy an instinct – though likely to be pleasurable in itself – would incur the risk of provoking unpleasure because of other requirements" (Laplanche and Pontalis 1988: 390).

7. I use the term "découpage" here mostly in the Bazinian spirit of the term that Timothy Barnard evokes in his updated translation of *What is Cinema?* For Barnard's Bazin, découpage is "editing's corollary at the mise-en-scène stage of production" and a way of "organizing the profilmic" (2009: 265, 279). Bazin has also referred to découpage as "composition and camera movement" (2009: 264) and as "the aesthetic of the relationship between shots" (as they are conceived, Barnard tells us, not as they are edited) (2009: 264). Elsewhere, Noël Burch (1981: 4) has described découpage as the "underlying structure of the finished film", which Barnard argues should in fact be called "formal treatment" (2009: 264). In spite of Burch's apparent blindness to the fact that the process of découpage starts long before the film is finished and can be used to discuss creative aspects of film production, Burch's notion of "underlying structure" best encapsulates how découpage can be seen and felt in a film. In the following analysis my use of the term then borrows from both Burch and Barnard as I use the term to speak simultaneously of the film's underlying formal structure (of which editing certainly plays a part in determining), its shot composition, as well as the aesthetic relationship between shots as they are conceived and then edited in line with this guiding directorial vision. I opt to

analyze the film's "découpage" rather than solely its "editing" be-cause "découpage" holds onto the importance of shot composition (which is inextricable from how a film like this is structured and later edited) and also because it recognizes that the film's underlying structure is given birth in the filmmaker's mind before being shot, and that the editing of the film is then carried out in line with this original vision, in order to actualize it, rather than suppress it, by cutting it up into short takes that are easily digested by the commercial spectator.

8. *Découpage en plan américain* refers to the logic of shot organization at work in classical Hollywood studio era productions. See the chapter on découpage in David Bordwell's *History of Film Style* (1997) for a discussion of this term (which contrasts quite sharply with Timothy Barnard's later usage of the term découpage in Bazin 2009).

9. For Deleuze, the outside is "always an opening onto a future [where] nothing ends, since nothing has begun, but everything is trans-formed" (Deleuze 1988: 89).

10. While the opacity of the outside may not be a background, it nevertheless "re-introduces ambiguity into the structure of the image", which for Bazin is one of the defining traits of *découpage en profond-eur* (1997: 101).

11. Reality is here understood in a different sense than it often acquires within film studies discussions of realism. In these discussions, what scholars who use the term reality really mean, is a more specialized notion of the term that could be called "profilmic reality". Profilmic reality is a term that comes from the work of Étienne Souriau and refers to the world that exists before the camera, which the camera then records (see Souriau's *L'Univers filmique* (1953: 8). When I use the term reality here, I am speaking of an entirely different relation-ship between image and reality. What interests me is not how the camera adheres to a profilmic reality, or even how the camera is productive of reality (which studies of direct cinema documentaries have so frequently pointed out), but that the reality of the image is informed by ontological functors. The Fluxes of the image are really the only domain that exists in a reciprocal relationship with the profilmic reality. Values, Phlya, and the existential Territories of the self remain sensuously imperceptible, yet all still go into produc-ing the reality of the image – what it really contains, what it really

expresses, what it really does, and what effects it may really produce in the world.

12. Erin Manning deploys the term relational movement to emphasize movement's metastable and creative quality of "worlding". For Manning, the relational movement of bodies in space literally creates the world in which the movement happens (creates the world *through* movement). For a discussion on relational movement, see Manning (2009). I use the term here to emphasize how the creative act of bringing a world into existence emerges immanent to the movement of the ontological functors at work in a given event, and how the body always carries these functors into the event via the very fact of its existence, and its potential for prompting movements in others that can invoke resubjectifying affects.

13. For Guattari's original chart that lays out the co-compositions between actual and real, and virtual and possible in the ontological quantrants, see page 28 of *Schizoanalytic Cartographies* (2013).

14. Thus Apichatpong's ecosophic aesthetic composition reflects what Brian Massumi has to say about how the entirety of the event always contains a nonsensuous component. "Even if the event's conditioning elements and culmination are actual, the entirety of the event is virtual: doubly nonlocal, nonsensuously present, registering only in effect, and on all three counts really abstract" (Massumi 2011: 24).

15. Some of these other films that use imagery similar to that found in Boonmee's dream sequence include the various shorts that make up *The Primitive Project* (2009), such as *A Letter to Uncle Boonmee* (2009) and *Phantoms of Nabua* (2009).

16. Apichatpong explains the pertinence of his cinematic intervention into the contemporary Thai mediascape as follows: "The story of Nabua undeniably has echoes of the current political turmoil in Thailand. Institutions involved in those events of the past, along with new ones, are the key players in the ongoing chaos. Just as in the past, they manipulate the public psyche, instilling it with faith and fear" (Weerasethakul 2009a: 198). In the same piece he provides a further account of how he encountered the stories of Nabua's military occupation while filming his *Letter to Uncle Boonmee* for the *Primitive* project.

17. Actual occasions are the "final real things of which the world is made up", they are "drops of experience, complex and interdependent"

(Whitehead 1978: 27). Actual occasions emerge from process, and thus carry a selective function, for they never actualize all of the possibilities offered by the processual flow from one set of actual occasions to another.

18. Whitehead might have even considered *Uncle Boonmee* a historical adventure film, given its activation of the past: "[A]dventures are to the adventurous [...] a passive knowledge of the past loses the whole value of its message" (Whitehead 1967: 279).

Works Cited

Alpern, Stephen I. "Insurgency in Northeast Thailand: A New Cause for Alarm". *Asian Survey* 15.8 (August 1975): 684–92.

Bazin, André. *What is Cinema?* Trans. Timothy Barnard. Montreal: Caboose, 2009. 261-281.

Benjamin, Walter. "Theses on the Philosophy of History". *Illuminations*. New York: Schocken Books, 1969: 253–64.

Boehler, Natalie. "The Jungle as Border Zone: The Aesthetics of Nature in the Work of Apichatpong Weerasethakul". *ASEAS – Austrian Journal of South-East Asian Studies* 4.2 (2011): 290–304.

Bordwell, David. *On the History of Film Style*. Cambridge, MA: Harvard University Press, 1997.

Burch, Noël. *Theory of Film Practice*. Trans. Helen R. Lane. Princeton, NJ: Princeton University Press, 1981.

Casella, Alessandro. "Communism and Insurrection in Thailand". *The World Today* 26.5 (May 1970): 197–208.

Deleuze, Gilles. *Foucault*. Trans. Seán Hand. Minneapolis: University of Minnesota Press, 1988.

Deleuze, Gilles and Félix Guattari. *Anti-Oedipus: Capitalism and Schizophrenia, vol. 1*. Trans. Robert Hurley, Mark Seem and Helen R. Lane. Minneapolis: University of Minnesota Press, 1983.

Guattari, Félix. *Schizoanalytic Cartographies*. London and New York: Bloomsbury Academic, 2013.

Guattari, Félix. *The Three Ecologies*. London and New York: Continuum, 2008.

LaPlanche, Jean and Jean-Bertrand Pontalis. *The Language of Psychoanalysis*. Trans. Donald Nicholson-Smith. London: Karnac Books, 1988.

Manning, Erin. *Relationscapes: Movement, Art, Philosophy*. Cambridge, MA and London: The MIT Press, 2009.

Massumi, Brian. "Deleuze and Guattari's Theories of the Group-Subject, Through a Reading of Corneille's *Le Cid*". *Discours Social/Social Discourse* 1.4 (Winter 1988): 423–40.

Massumi, Brian. *Semblance and Event: Activist Philosophy and the Occurent Arts.* Cambridge, MA and London: The MIT Press, 2011.

Mullino Moore, Mary Elizabeth. "Imagine Peace: Knowing the Real – Imagining the Impossible". Ed. Jay B. McDaniel and Donna Bowman. *Handbook of Process Theology*. St. Louis, MO: Chalice, 2006: 201–16.

Quandt, James. Ed. *Apichatpong Weerasethakul*. Vienna: Synema Publikationen, 2009.

Rithdee, Kong. "Thailand Passes Controversial Film Act". *Variety*. Published December 20, 2007. Available from: http://variety.com/2007/film/news/thailand-passes-controversial-film-act-1117978081/ (accessed Septmber 12, 2016).

Rosen, Philip. "Nation and Anti-Nation: Concepts of National Cinema in the 'New' Media Era". *Diaspora* 5.3 (1996): 386–93.

Souriau, Ètienne. *L'Univers filmique*. Paris: Flammarion, 1953.

Stengers, Isabelle. "Beyond Conversation: The Risks of Peace". *Process and Difference: Between Cosmological and Poststructuralist Postmodernisms*. Ed. Catherine Keller and Anne Daniell. Albany: State University of New York Press, 2002: 235–55.

Thomas, M. Ladd. "Communist Insurgency in Thailand: Factors Contributing to Its Decline". *Asian Affairs* 13.1 (Spring, 1986): 17–26.

Watson, Janell. *Guattari's Diagrammatic Thought: Writing Between Lacan and Deleuze*. London and New York: Continuum, 2009.

Weerasethakul, Apichatpong. "The Memory of Nabua: A Note on the Primitive Project". *Apichatpong Weerasethakul*. Ed. James Quandt. Vienna: Synema Publikationen, 2009a: 192–206.

Weerasethakul, Apichatpong. "The Folly and Future of Thai Cinema Under Military Dictatorship". *Apichatpong Weerasethakul*. Ed. James Quandt. Vienna: Synema Publikationen, 2009b: 178–81.

Whitehead, Alfred North. *Adventures of Ideas*. New York and London: The Free Press, 1967.

Whitehead, Alfred North. *Process and Reality: An Essay in Cosmology*. New York and London: The Free Press, 1978.

Apichatpong has long been one of Tsai Ming-Liang's greatest admirers. Apart from the fact that they are both from Southeast Asia, the two filmmakers share a particular *care for opacity* that impregnates their cinematic gesture and suggests a common set of ethical and aesthetic concerns. The a-dramatic slowness that characterizes their cinema, as well as a multifaceted refusal of conventional narrative and drama questions our constituent relationship both with images and with the rapidly transforming spaces of global capitalism. These features contribute to the production a lasting impression of opacity. Following Aristotle's paradigmatic definition, drama is indeed an *elucidation* of a situation, a way to make it intelligible. What matters for them is, following Tsai's words, to "protect the obscurity of characters, relations and things". How should we envisage this elastically conservative filmic gesture? What kind of conceptual tools and analytical approaches are required in order for the obscure and the vague, for the "mysterious objects at noon" populating their cinema not be explained away? In what ways does their cinema resist to simply signify, in order to propose complex visual and temporal enigmas? How does it nourish zones of non-knowledge and inoperativeness and enter in the composition of renewed ecosophic assemblages?

To say that Apichatpong's cinema seeks to mystify us would be to misunderstand it. On the contrary, his cinema aims, right through the heart of the night, to let the world be, in all transparency. It is a cinema of trans-apparition.

In this sense, I think one must consider his cinema as an invitation to live life as an initiation. But an initiation into what? Not so much into a doctrine on the processuality of the world or the non-discursive dimension of the event, but as something closer to life itself, a life that is living, imaginal, haptic and gently enchanted.

Érik Bordeleau

Percolating the Elusive:
Into Apichatpong's Dreamscape

> The theory which I am urging admits a greater ultimate
> mystery and a deeper ignorance. The past and the
> future meet and mingle in the ill-defined present. The
> passage of nature which is only another name for
> the creative force of existence has no narrow ledge
> of definite instantaneous present within which to
> operate. Its operative presence which is now urging
> nature forward must be sought for throughout the
> whole, in the remotest past as well as in the narrowest
> breadth of any present duration. Perhaps also in the
> unrealised future. Perhaps also in the future which
> might be as well as the actual future which will be.
>
> *Alfred N. Whitehead (1920: 73)*

> Movies are a form of black magic. It's instinctive.
>
> *Apichatpong Weerasethakul (Pansittivorakul 2006)*

A Natural Aesthetics of Mystery

All things somber and mysterious, fantastic and animated
– such as the films of Apichatpong Weerasethakul – pose a
particular problem for those who want to approach them by
discursive means without mutilating them. One should of course
not further obscure them, nor treat them in a mystifying or

"obscurantist" manner; but it is just as important to not elucidate them unduly, and instead develop modes of presentation for them that preserve their relative opacity, their own ways of moving and proposing occasions of encounter. An enticing analysis envelops as much as it explains that which moves us about these things; it beckons us towards *experience*, in the wide and at once rigorous sense that radical empiricists have given that notion. Developed to its full potential by William James, Alfred North Whitehead or John Dewey, the concept of experience – "nothing but experience, but nothing less than experience," James would say – crosses the limits of consciousness or of subjectivity in order to reconfigure our relation to knowing and, perhaps even more so, to unknowing. That is how Whitehead can write without any intention to obfuscate that his concept of nature "admits a greater ultimate mystery and a deeper ignorance" and defines philosophy as a mystical activity that, in the name of a constant renewal of thought and society, explores the unsayable without ever renouncing the requirements of rationality (1968: 73).[1] For John Dewey, philosophy must similarly be wary of the simplicity of the clear and distinct which suits the categorical understanding so well. In a movement of thought that prefigures and justifies the spontaneously transdisciplinary and joyously undisciplined trajectories that characterize the practice of research-creation, Dewey invites us to refrain from hastily dismissing the vague and dark elements that fill experience and to be attentive to the potentials they comprise.[2]

I would like to address the cinema of Apichatpong and more specifically his *Primitive* project in this "naturalist" mindset. In dialogue with his films and the fascinating and elusive images that populate his cinema, these philosophical considerations on the empiricist and speculative conception of experience and its relation to the passage of nature as a creative force suggest something like a natural aesthetic of mystery or, by extension, a mystic nature of the aesthetic. How can one avoid explaining

Fig. 30: Still from *Uncle Boonmee*.

away in the name of legibility the vague and distinct-obscure that persists in all of our aesthetic experiences? How to account for that unknown element in them which interpellates and draws us in, often without our knowing why? Perhaps it has to do with their *allure*, the more or less virtual movement that adorns certain things or people with an unprecedented propositional power. For the word "allure" points toward the singular manner that courses through a being and characterizes it: a sort of evanescent signature – a style – charged with a force of affective propulsion that invites further folds and relays. But conversely, the word also reveals an interplay of capture and enthrallment, how the captivating allure acts as a *lure for feeling*. This idea of a propositional efficacy that stands in direct relation to the sensible is at the heart of Whitehead's philosophy. It concerns the way in which a proposition, aesthetic or otherwise, acts as an attractor for new feelings and as a vector for new becomings. Indeed, for Whitehead, any propositional feeling is an occasion for the modification of experience, for a bifurcation that could potentially create an event or be taken up again later. As Isabelle Stengers writes in her monumental *Thinking with Whitehead*, "the entertainment [of propositions] lures us into feeling, thinking, speaking, in short, becomes, in the most various ways, an ingredient of the experiences that will follow it" (2011a: 418). Stengers takes great care to specify that the proposition itself does not explain the "entertainment" through which it comes into existence. That is the reason why there is mystery and excess, "deeper ignorance" and encounter, with all the openness, contingency and indetermination this implies.

Like the term *agencement*, which suggests at the same time the elegance of what is well assembled and the underlying work of arranging heterogeneous elements, the word "allure" evokes at once what may be called the *super-natural* ease of a successful envelopment and, beneath the surface, the fine material constellation that the interplay of captures establishes, through which becomings effectively pass. Exploring the propositional efficacy of Apichatpong's soulful filmic gesture, I wish to focus more specifically on the importance he confers to the notion of the dream in his cinematic practice and its ethopoietic effects.

A Fantasy that Wants Nothing More Than to Make Night Fall into the Day

> Despite your efforts to avoid having to evoke light in speaking of the obscure...
>
> *Maurice Blanchot (1993: 31)*

Apichatpong says that cinema is a form of black magic, that it is essentially instinctive. Indeed, his cinema operates and submerges us in the "subtle element": he develops a manner all his own to make reality appear and disappear, to refine the real by means of cinema's specific propensity towards the oneiric. Apichatpong's cinema puts things into a mode of suspension: it brims with virtual and fleeting states, transitory twilight worlds where the living and the dead meet, and even moments of carnal grace (think of the sublime insouciance of *Blissfully Yours* and the languor of *Mekong Hotel*). He seems entirely devoted to making us experience the imperceptible meanderings of time's passage, the unstable and indefinite nature of the present.

Apichatpong's cinema seems like a marvelous response to Blanchot's subtle interrogation: how to discover the obscure without uncovering it? Few are the filmmakers who understand so well how to film both the jungle and the night, asking us in the gentlest of ways to give ourselves over to them so that they may eventually pass through us. An active mediation of the obscure-to-be-lived; mysterious passivity of a lived immediacy. The tropical mist – or cloud – of unknowing[3] that engulfs all of Apichatpong's films invites *contemplation* in the creative sense that Deleuze and Guattari have given the term: "Contemplating is creating, the mystery of passive creation, sensation. Sensation fills out the plane of composition and is filled with itself by filling itself with what it contemplates: it is 'enjoyment' and 'self-enjoyment'" (1994: 212).[4] This mystery of passive creation is an essential ingredient of any *active* relation to the future or, more precisely, to futurity. In a comment on this crucial passage of *What is Philosophy?*, Giorgio Agamben emphasizes the necessity to conceive obscurity not simply as an absence or removal of light but as something that one must be able to produce and articulate – a wander line or, as mystics refer to it, a "night of the soul".[5]

Tilda Swinton describes with moving sharpness the transparent and unassuming mystery that pervades the films of Apichatpong, the call to (impersonally) experience the night as forest and the forest as night. What is at stake for the famous actress is cinema considered as vector for a life initiated to the refined charms of involuntarism:

> I wish I could show my children these films, although I know we won't for some years. I feel they would settle them, give them a *divining rod for the future*, when

> the light might trick them into thinking editing is the
> answer to a sense of real power in life.
>
> But I am patient. It's bigger children that need
> *these archeological remnants of sentient – cohesive –*
> *possibilities, of post-choice harmony*, these reminders
> of the natural order of gesture, of faith, of acceptance.
> [...] The forest binds the soul and holds it, safe and
> wild, in his cinema. I am deeply besotted with that
> particular wilderness. (Cousins and Swinton 2009: 11,
> emphasis added)

This quotation offers a number of leads towards the threshold of the future anterior and of ethopoietics to which I will return in the last section of this essay. Suffice it to say for now that Swinton gracefully links present, future and past in an archaeological gesture carried by a harmony that resorbs, at least partially, the excesses of voluntarism that modern En*light*enment has encouraged. This is about an art of immanent attention that knows how to resist causal narratives that simply make the present follow on from the past, a resistance that allows events to come from their virtual beginnings: a future that is always already implicated and whose effects one must anticipate, not unlike a diviner. The real is immanently recharged with the fantastic on this subtle and necessarily elusive threshold, this wild, nocturnal fringe through which spirits – and not only those that pass through the films of Apichatpong – are always to come, always coming about. As discrete but nonetheless insisting events, they effectively *complicate* our relation to time; they mark a territory and call upon the multiple. The nocturnal and forestial effect of Apichatpong's cinema resides in this patient and attentive *disposition of spirits*.

"Perhaps cinema is never as fantastic as when the ghost, before materializing in a body, can already be felt, when the invisible is hardly perceptible" (Leutrat 1995: 59). In Apichatpong's cinema,

Fig. 31: Construction of the spaceship.

the invisible gathers in secret; spectres come and go, without tragedy or terror. They participate in a "subtle fantastic, one that has no regard for supernatural manifestations and turns the real, the ordinary, the everyday into an apparition, an epiphany, a ghost, indeed, into a shrouded cadaver" (Leutrat 199: 101). If Apichatpong assigns such a determining role to the night – the time of metamorphoses and transformations *par excellence* – he also takes great care to remind us that ghosts only appear under conditions of liminality, specifically "at the break of dawn and twilight" (Weerasethakul 2009: 192). Apichatpong's films are recognizable for being both initiatory and fundamentally a-dramatic, for the modest way in which they make night fall into the day in order to activate the minimal, liminal and potentially magical threshold of cinema.

The *Primitive* Project

> The power of dreaming is a divine and mysterious
> power. It is through dreaming that man communicates
> with the dark dream by which he is surrounded.
>
> *Charles Baudelaire (1971: 148)*

Fig. 32: Spaceship flying at the break of dawn and twilight.

Uncle Boonmee Who Can Recall His Past Lives is part of a larger project called *Primitive* that includes an installation of the same title, two short films – *A Letter to Uncle Boonmee* and *Phantoms of Nabua* – as well as an artist book. The project, which addresses questions of extinction and memory, is set in the northeast of Thailand, a region that has experienced a strong anti-communist repression. In an interview with James Quandt, Apichatpong confides that it was none other than Benedict Anderson who persuaded him to travel through Thailand's northeast to explore the tormented history of his home region.

From the 1950s to the early '80s, communists coming from Vietnam and Laos settled in this part of the country. In the '60s, Nabua had effectively become a "red zone" and, with American support, the Thai government gradually intensified its operations against a local population considered too sympathetic towards the interests of the enemy. The repression was brutal and many peasants had to flee into the jungle to escape the atrocities. *Uncle Boonmee* refers directly to these acts of violence. For instance, Boonmee himself says that the disease from which he suffers is a result of his bad karma, of having killed too many communists. The *Primitive* project is also grounded in Apichatpong's concern for the political troubles that have recently shaken Thailand. He has repeatedly expressed his rather pessimistic vision for the future of his country and been increasingly involved in the fight against film censorship. And yet, he has often pointed out that he does not consider himself particularly politicized and that cinema is for him first and foremost a means of personal expression.

In light of this, the *Primitive* project can be legitimately seen as a poetic and cinematographic attempt at documenting and archiving the memory of a tormented past that is in danger of disappearing entirely. But such a reading would fail to properly grasp what is really at stake in this oeuvre. For, instead of collecting the memories of people who have lived these traumatic events themselves, Apichatpong has decided to focus his attention on the life of the teenagers who live in the village of Nabua. He says:

> Everywhere we went there were stories. Helicopter shot down here, friends shot there, beheadings happened bere. Gradually, just standing in this quiet land became an intense experience for me. Perhaps too intense, for I doubted I was in the right place. [...] For me, the presence of the teens had made Nabua's air breathable. Soon *Primitive* became a portrait of the teenage male descendants of the farmer communists, freed from the widow ghost's empire. (Weerasethakul 2009: 198)

Curiously, one of the principal elements of the project consists in constructing a spaceship in collaboration with the teenage villagers. Apichatpong has been fascinated by science-fiction for a long time. "I always dreamed of making a movie with a spaceship. When could there be a better time to do so than now in Thailand? And somehow Nabua is a perfect place for this vehicle to land and to introduce the idea of a journey" (Weerasethakul 2009: 200). The spaceship incarnates dimensions of the fantastic and futurity that effectively complicate a more conventional relation to the past than we would expect from an artwork that is interested in suppressed memories. Much like the fresh and youthful air that Apichatpong appreciates in Nabua's adolescents, the spaceship brings fresh air and allows for a liberating relation with history. As Karen Newman suggests, his spaceships "give us time and space to re-dream the past and ask what can be learned to create a better future for the next generation" (Newman 2009: 152). It is this dreamed relation between the past, the present and the future – the transformative and transductive dreamscape in which his project unfolds – that is crucial to Apichatpong's work and is what I would like to explore further. Is the dream not a vague and mysterious operator capable of inducing new becomings? Is it not the essential component of a speculative filmic gesture towards new possibilities of existence?

Cinema as an Extension of the Soul

> … an art is never just an art; at the same time it is always a suggested world.
>
> *Jacques Rancière (2014: 38)*

Several filmmakers have described the great proximity between cinema and the oneiric dimension of existence. Pasolini for example has spoken of cinema's power to embody dreams. But to my knowledge, even if Abbas Kiorastami welcomes the fact that people fall asleep during the projection of his films, nobody (besides perhaps David Lynch?) has gone as far as Apichatpong in exploring the oneiric dimension of cinema. One can affirm without too much risk that, together with the ghost, the dream is the principal notion that describes Apichatpong's cinematographic project and around which his poetic relation to history and the entangled dimensions of time are articulated. Discussing the *Primitive* project, he affirms:

> The teenagers provided me with the future of the
> place. When I went there, it was very much like a
> performance: you don't know what to do. You just go
> there and work with them to create dreams. *In dreams
> you can't take control.* So it's like a collaborative dream-
> making. (Kim 2011: 50, emphasis added)

Here, the dream appears as an elusive space that escapes
voluntary control and in which everyone's existence and
desires potentially attune to each other's. To dream, then,
is to reach a point where reality ceases to be a principle, to
enter a space in which it becomes possible to elaborate and
resonate in collective harmonies as yet unknown. Those
who follow the open trajectories of a dream surely open
themselves to new possibilities, but they also run the risk of a
fundamental questioning, if not a radical derealization. Perhaps
we are protecting ourselves against just this possibility, as
the anthropologist Eduardo Viveiros de Castro has poignantly
suggested in his critique of speculative realism's negative
anthropocentrism. Quoting his friend during the Cerisy
conference on Speculative Gesture (2013), the shaman Ravi
Kopenauer, he says, "White people sleep a lot but only dream
about themselves". And perhaps it is better this way or,
differently put, perhaps it is a welcome protective measure
because, following Deleuze, the dream is a site for terrible
predations. It is better to dream of oneself than not to dream
at all, he seems to tell us in his talk "What is the Creative Act?"
from 1987, to the extent that it protects us against the dreams
of others. For "as soon as someone else dreams, there is
danger. People's dreams are always all-consuming and threaten
to devour us" (Deleuze 2006: 318). In short, then, what the
dream puts at stake is the becoming of our soul itself. We have
been warned.

There is indeed no veritable dream that isn't also shaped by
the danger of losing one's foothold. And this is precisely the

condition *sine qua non* for an existential transformation, the price at which the fragile and hazardous possibility of being initiated into the dreams of others takes form. In the last pages of *Thinking with Whitehead*, Isabelle Stengers evokes these interstices in which all our dreams meet anonymously, far from any regulated representations and watchwords:

> only dreamers can accept the modification of
> their dream. [...] And if the exchange is possible, if
> sometimes – an essentially anonymous event – one
> dream may induce the modification of another or
> evoke another, it is insofar as their point of junction
> is always a tangent point: neither a frontal clash
> between rival powers nor being swallowed up in the
> other's dream, not confusion in a banal dream of
> power but a local resonance, designating past tenses
> of divergent accomplishments and future tenses
> responding to distinct tests. (Stengers 2011: 516–8)

This opens up a number of avenues for thought. I am interested first of all in the way in which the dream appears as the site for a differential gathering in which dissimilar elements come together and find the possibility for a new assemblage. The local entering into resonance of which Stengers speaks is a communication between heterogeneous elements; and one easily perceives in the quoted passage how important it is to her that none of the elements that the dreams put into variation ever enter a simple process of collective fusion. This properly cosmopolitical concern corresponds to "the problematic co-presence of practices [...]: the experience, always in the present, of the one into whom the other's dreams, doubts, hopes, and fears pass" (Stengers 2011a: 372).

The dream as defined by Stengers constitutes a determining component of any assemblage charged with metamorphic potential. It offers the – literal and not at all metaphoric

Fig. 33: Still from *Cemetery of Splendour*.

– possibility of a composition among beings and that which in them, more or less voluntarily, on the distinct-obscure threshold of their desires, offers itself up to the encounter. But how does Apichatpong's dream and those of Nabua's teenagers pass into us? Through cinema, of course, the art of which Deleuze and Guattari rightly said has a particular aptitude to capture the birth of deliriums and the burgeoning of events "precisely because it is not analytical and regressive, but explores a global field of coexistence" (1983: 274). Apichatpong's precious remark concerning the relation between dream and cinema must be understood along these lines, with all the required technical considerations:

> [Thus cinema can be a phantom in this sense]:
> because it's something that you really need to dream.
> Cinema is a vehicle we produce for ourselves and
> as part of us. It's like an extension of our soul that
> manifests itself. (Kim 2011: 52)

This assertion confirms the general impression one gathers from Apichatpong's films, namely that in his films dream and cinema are actively thrown into a relation of reciprocal indetermination.

This explains, if only in part, the contagious potential of his cinema, its unique ability to profoundly modify the entirety of our perceptions. It is through dreaming the medium of cinema and making it reach [unprecedented degrees of defocalisation[6] that Apichatpong manages to operate directly on the subtle element], creating atmospheres that affect our understanding of the distinction between the real and the imaginary as well as coax our relation to the visible and the invisible along new and unexpected directions.

We are now able to problematize in more detail the tense relationhip between dreaming and the suffocating effect of the positivity of history, as described by Apichatpong with regard to his choice of working mainly with the teenagers of Nabua. This relation is particularly complex in Apichatpong's cinema to the extent that it implies, as with any great filmmaker, a reflection on cinema as a technical medium as well as a profoundly existential dimension that *effectively* concerns our soul. Or rather: in Apichatpong, the reflection on the medium is practically speaking indiscernible from the spiritual considerations that never fail to astound and which some of our critical habits would rather leave aside. At exactly this point, the tradition of speculative pragmatism, with its expanded conception of experience, is of great help. What does Apichatpong mean to say when he affirms that cinema is "a part of us" and that it is "an extension of our soul that manifests itself"? One might think at first glance that he simply wants to say that cinema is for us a way of expressing ourselves. But express what exactly? Our "interiority"? Our "emotions"? Our "soul"? Via a detour through Buddhism, Apichatpong's cinematographic practice reveals itself to be as immanentist as possible, rejoining the Deleuzian idea according to which "the brain is the screen" (Deleuze 2006: 282). Indeed, Apichatpong is particularly fond of the following anecdote that James Quandt has chosen to place on the inside cover of the book on Apichatpong that he edited:

> A monk recently told me that meditation was like filmmaking. He said when one meditates, one doesn't need film. As if film was an excess. In a way he is right. *Our brain is the best camera and projector. If only we can find a way to operate it properly.* (Quandt 2009: 184, emphasis added)[7]

When Deleuze pronounced his by now famous statement – "the brain is the screen" – he had in mind the developments in molecular biology which he opposed to the linguistic and psychoanalytical models of film analysis. Eager to establish a continuum between the spectator's brain and the cinema screen, he meant to foreground the way in which moving images trace and retrace, immediately so to speak, our brain circuits.[8] In a curious reversal, the image of thought that Apichatpong proposes also indirectly echoes recent developments in neuroscience, which is interested in solving the mystery of the beneficial effects that meditative practices have on the functioning of the brain. Incidentally, Apichatpong says he has always been interested in the activity of the human mind and that he is working on a film in which the characters fall prey to a sleeping sickness.[9] This will serve as an occasion to explore the influence of daylight on memory and dreams.

But at first glance nothing indicates that this remark of Apichatpong's is in the least compatible with the cuts and connections of Deleuze and Guattari's machinic animism[10] or even with a more conventional exploration of the relation between cinema and the cognitive sciences. On the contrary, its spiritualizing tenor suggests that cinema as media technology is simply superfluous. If only we were able to plunge deep enough into ourselves, if only our relation to the world wasn't so distorted and alienated, we wouldn't need any memorial support or external projection organ – in short, we could dispense with the cinematic apparatus. This is, in essence, what the Buddhist monk seems to say and to which Apichatpong seems to acquiesce: we humans are admittedly prosthetic beings but this could surely be otherwise, provided that we find the path towards an integral use of our spiritual faculties. This apparently conservative, even reactionary attitude towards media technologies is only reinforced by Apichatpong's mixed feelings with regard to the relation between Buddhism and cinema. Indeed, right before the above-cited interview passage, he confides: "I have this conflicting feeling because sometimes I think filmmaking contradicts Buddhism. It is not about looking into yourself, but about making an illusion of that process" (Quandt 2009: 184). But if we can resist ever so slightly our bad academic habits of sending Apichatpong's scruples to the pillory of critical posthuman transformism, perhaps a new perspective will reveal itself that is able to enrich our various ecologies of practices, including the spiritual and the media-technological. For this purpose, one must be willing to take Apichatpong's concerns seriously. And what exactly does he say? That the cinema as an artistic practice which approaches introspection can harm the soul, for the soul is defined by the risk of its loss. It can be torn, dispersed, reduced, forgotten. It can also be saved. The soul and its incessant refocusing. To have a soul is to confront the improbable challenge of envisioning new possibilities to populate the present and to make life habitable. The soul, as it is understood here, has nothing substantial – if by that it is meant that it contains a stable and immutable core which is capable of holding itself and returning (I will shortly come back to the specific consistency of the movement of return). The soul is *essential* in the dynamic and monadological sense of the term in that it designates a minimum of belonging, a threshold of locality, a differential vulnerability – the expressive interiority of a fold.[11] In the vocabulary of speculative pragmatism, the "[s]oul is a mode of functioning that occasionally happens, not the ultimate truth of our experience" (Stengers 2005: 53–4).[12] In other words and as Whitehead has pointed out with his usual sobriety and rigor, we *become* souls – in this regard, there is no doubt

that Apichatpong's cinematographic propositions contribute
to this becoming in a utterly fantastic and unprecedented way.
From this perspective, the soul testifies to the fact that we are
(becoming) capable of entertaining possibilities as such, with
all their corollary doubts, hopes, excitations and hesitations. It
is proof that we find ourselves in a position to encounter and
entertain propositions as so many abstractions to be lived,
as so many *lived abstractions*: "The soul is not defined by its
limitations, but rather by what I'd call 'leaps of the imagination';
not community of intuition or appropriation, but becomings
triggered by something that cannot explain them, by the
proliferation experienced as such of these existants that are
propositions" (Stengers 2011b: 442).[13] Thus, following speculative
pragmatism, to take care of oneself and of one's soul is first of
all to care for one's modes of abstraction. Cinema is as much
a mode of abstraction as meditation.[14] And one can approach
either one from their mystical aspect if only one accepts that the
mystical is always already a matter of techniques of existence
with their very own possibilities for affective fullness and
attunement. Incidentally, Peirce seems to suggest something
of this order when he affirms that "[t]he greatest point of art
consists in the introduction of suitable abstractions" (quoted in
Massumi 2011: 15).

It seems to me that it is only within this expanded conceptual
frame, which integrates technical and spiritual considerations,
that we can do justice to the propositional efficacy contained
in the spiritual vision that Apichatpong proposes through the
anecdote of the Buddhist monk. His filmic gesture is ultimately
a matter of *returning* into history/in time – the specific and
even paradoxical challenge, falling to all of us, of conceiving this
retrospective and, at least seemingly, nostalgic movement as a
particular mode of abstraction. In other words, it is a matter of
providing oneself with the means for a technical and speculative
treatment of the question of returning, both ethopoietically
(going back as the essential "sedentary" component of a

becoming-soul and a self-caring refrain) and cinematographically (cinema as a time machine). For, as the name already indicates, at the heart of the *Primitive* project is the expression of a desire to return cinema to its origins, "before the image moved, before it became the moving image"; what discloses itself there and then, Apichatpong tells us, is "a kind of unraveling of the apparatus to a time before technology mediated how people remember and relate to the past" (Carrion-Murayari and Gioni 2011: 26).

So if Apichatpong highly values the image of a brain that is at the same time screen and projector, it is because this image nurtures the possibility, realized within the *Primitive* project (if only by way of the diversity of media employed), of de-creating cinema in order to reconnect with a time before moving images. The promise of spiritual plenitude resulting from the optimal use of our mental faculties that the Buddhist thought-image lets us glimpse creates space for a reflection on the cinematographic medium and its complex and entangled relation to time. It acts as a lure for feeling that induces a disjunctive dreaming which corresponds, not unlike a dark precursor of intimacy, to the delicate disposition of spirits that Apichatpong orchestrates in his cinema.

Apichatpong's cinema is about the fabrication of souls and spiritual conducts. The slow and powerful gesture of return that he establishes in the flow of moving images all the way to the historical threshold of the stilled frame, and the enigmatic doublings that proliferate at various moments of his cinema, constitute as many procedures for multiplying oneiric vortices and other abodes for the soul. It is from exactly this point of view, that of a machinic animism that is equally attached to the specificity of its medium and the possibility to dream this medium, that Apichatpong confronts the technological transformations that affect his practice, at a healthy distance from the foolishness of critical technophilia as well as any concealed nostalgia.

> Cinema is a vehicle we produce for ourselves and
> as part of us. It's like an extension of our soul that
> manifests itself. Concerning new technology, the soul
> is changing and I don't think it's naturally good or bad
> way. It's just changing and we need to pay attention
> to how it influences cinema. I don't make a strict
> judgment of what's going to die in cinema. I wanted
> to express my longing for the old Thai cinema in
> Uncle Boonmee, but my aim was less to revive the old
> cinema itself, than invite the audience to realize what
> was there before. (Kim 2011:52)

The Archeological Gesture as a Use of
Going Back and Forth

> BUT the Future is only dark from the outside. *Leap* into
> it – and it EXPLODES with *Light*.
> *Mina Loy (1996: 149)*

> Returning is being *but only the being of becoming*.
> *Deleuze (1994: 41)[15]*

In the previously quoted excerpt from her letter to Mark Cousin, Tilda Swinton evokes through her inspired prose the ethopoietic effects of the wild obscurity that envelops Apichatpong's cinema. His films preserve within their depths a reserve of night to be "discovered without being uncovered", archeological and virtual sheets of time to be approached with the circumspection of the diviner, as zones of unknowing that carry new sentient possibilities so that we may resist the temptation of *life editing* and the overly clear cuts of the will. It's as if, to speak with Giorgio Agamben, "this invisible light that is the darkness of the present", the very same that emanates from the films of Apichatpong, "cast its shadow on the past, so that the past, touched by this shadow, acquired the ability to respond to the darkness of the now" (2009a: 53). Thus, the cinema of Apichatpong would

Fig. 34: Still from *Phantoms of Nabua*.

possess the remarkable power to transform into seers those who are disposed to be interpellated by its transparent mystery, to make them more attentive to the thin spiritual veneer that laces their gestures and to the share of the unlived that persists in them; in short, to make them, in as gentle a way as possible, contemporaries. "And to be contemporary means in this sense to return to a present where we have never been" (Agamben 2009a: 51–2). But is this even possible?

By way of conclusion, I would like to take up once more the question of the dream as return and path to self-enjoyment by engaging one of the very first publications of Michel Foucault, namely the introduction to the French translation of *Dream and Existence* by the phenomenological psychiatrist Ludwig Binswanger. This text, published in 1954 and revisited by Agamben in the context of his reflection on the archeological gesture in *The Signature of All Things*, is dense and complex. It discusses anthropology's relation to the image and signification, and proposes a critical step beyond phenomenology that already anticipates the subsequent development of Foucault's work. One of the passages that is crucial for my interpretation of

Apichatpong's filmic dreamscape and the creative tension that it establishes with the positive element of history, reads as follows:

> *All imagination, to be authentic, must once more learn to dream*, and "ars poetica" has no meaning unless it teaches us to break with the fascination of images and to reopen, for imagination, its path of freedom toward the dream that offers it, as its absolute truth, the "irrefragable kernel of night." [...] Purified in the fire of the dream, [...] The image is no longer image of something, totally projected toward an absence which it replaces; rather, it is gathered into itself and is given as the fullness of a presence; it doesn't denote something anymore, *it is addressed to someone.* [...] Not that the dream is the truth of history. But in *bringing forth that which in Existence is most irreducible to history*, the dream shows best the meaning it can take [...]. (Foucault 1984–85: 73–44, emphasis added; slightly modified)

The dream as Foucault describes it participates in the emergence of a freedom for the end of *a* world. The present is addressed by it. This foregrounds the speculative and propositional presence of the dream which, in its radical inactuality, calls forth a becoming towards an as yet unnamed hour. For "purified in the fire of the dream," as Foucault tells us, the image no longer acts as a simple designation or recall: it becomes itself the occasion for a fulfillment. As fire takes hold of a being, the dream sweeps up the composition of residual images as a form of life to extract from it a new incandescence, a new possibility of existence. How could one not, in this context, think of the magnificent short film *Phantoms of Nabua*? It shows a screen in the night onto which lightning is projected. In the twilight of the screen, the teenagers of Nabua gradually appear, playing soccer with a burning football. Every time it is hit, the flying ball produces a powerful hypnotic rustle. The screen eventually lights up in flames, thus laying bare the ghostly light of the projector in the night and a spectator distraught by so much radiance and intensity.

The dream as a "de-actualized peak of the present" interpolates the course of history and releases an unprecedented contemporaneity (Deleuze 1989: 130). It presents itself as the transindividual space and jouissance of a *more-to-live* – the effect of an affective propulsion that inheres to the oneiric plenitude in all its incandescent futurity. In the way it addresses the liveliness that coasts through us, then, the dream is a "natural" creative force and in this sense it is "irreducible to history". But this address is nothing less than paradoxical to the extent that it is most often indirect, elusive, and even impersonal. As if the proper content of the dream or the reverie, its "irrefragable kernel of night" as René Char has it, must remain anonymous, impenetrable, and never become a *matter of concern*, must never concern us. As if the dream – Apichatpong's, in this case – could just as well not take hold of us and move us, and not only because it can only reach us by way of the uncertain grace of its cinematographic articulation. The archeological gesture indicates the essentially *precarious* quality of the dream as element of an art of existence.

Uncle Boonmee Who Can Recall His Past Lives tells the story of man afflicted with a kidney disease and whose end is nearing. His imminent death invokes numerous ghosts and spirits that emerge one after the other, as if their presence made palpable the threshold between the living and the dead. With softness and simplicity, the film induces a sense of floatation and reverie, as we drift from one previous life to the next as so many unlived pasts or potential lives of which it matters little in the end to whom they must be attributed. Through this remarkable effect of an a-subjective decentering, the limit between human and animal or the individual and its environment is naturally erased, following the principle of a "transmigration of souls between humans, plants, animals, and ghosts," as Apichatpong points

out in the director's statement that accompanies *Primitive*.
In this eminently porous, fluid and marvelously ecosophical
world, modes of address multiply and entangle, they compose
a fantastic and lush pluriverse in which each element, real or
imaginary, constitutes a new perspective; a superior plane of the
transindividual on which evolve those beings who, as Frédéric
Neyrat formulates in a beautiful reflection on the fantastic and
the "constitution of *our* outsides", "have passed from the world's
tearing apart to the life cinematographic" (Neyrat 2013).

At the moment of his death, Uncle Boonmee and his family
withdraw into a cave. He is caught in a strange vision: a dystopian
world to come in which some kind of authority has the power to
make "people from the past" disappear by shining a light at them.
As this vision is narrated in a voice-over, a series of immobile
images interpolate the course of the film. They are troubling
and rather low-fi photographs that show a group of teenagers
dressed in military uniforms and proudly posing with a ghost
they have just caught (which, as in the rest of the film, takes
the form of a gorilla). One can recognize them as the illustrious
adolescents of Nabua although viewers who do not know the
rest of the *Primitive* project would not know. Boonmee explains
in voice-over that "[t]he light projected images from their past
onto a screen until their arrival in the future. Once these images
appeared, these 'past people' disappeared".

How is this rather mysterious allegory of a disappearance by
means of photographic or cinematographic projection to be
understood? Does cinema not, to the contrary, have the capacity
to conserve better than any other art the traces and presence
of the past? Apichatpong provides us with an important clue
for solving this riddle when he points out that this sequence of
the film unfolds from the perspective of a future of the past or,
differently put, from a future anterior. This indicates once more
the convergence of his reflection on the filmic medium and his
remarkable conception of the dream, as well as their mutual

impact on our ways of relating to the history of the present and to times past. Interviewed about this sequence, he says:

> For me, it's the place where Uncle Boonmee and I merge, because what he's talking about is my dream. […] it's about the future, but at the same time it has connotations of the present. In a way, we live in a totalitarian regime in Thailand, so I wanted to refer to this moment where the maker and the character merge. And when Uncle Boonmee goes back to the womb in the cave *I wanted to take the movie back to its origins, before the image moved, before it became the moving image.* […] There is a reference to the future, which is what Chris Marker talks about, but it's the future of the past. It's the representation of the future but from the past perspective. I'm very interested in these kinds of time shifts. (Sélavy 2010; emphasis added)

This problematization of the present through the "future of the past" corresponds point by point to Agamben's conception of the archeological gesture. The latter does not consist in the uncovering of factual truths of the past that one would only need to bring to the attention of the present; nor is it about unearthing buried memories for the sake of exposing them to the light of actuality – the allegory staged by Apichatpong shows with sufficient eloquence that this process of "illumination" or of a straightforward elucidation is inefficient, if not destructive. The archeological gesture does not aspire to a restoration of the historical moment because the *arche* that it aims at can never be fully identified with a specific moment in a chronological past. The arche in question does not represent a datum or a chronologically dated substance but rather a tension that traverses the element of history and that persists imperceptibly across the circumstances and modalities that have constituted it as an origin. In this sense, the archeological gesture, as it is defined by Agamben in *The Signature of All Things*, is the only access to the present: "Archaeology moves backward through the course of history [...] toward the point where history (whether individual or collective) becomes accessible for the first time, in accordance with the temporality of the future anterior" (2009b: 107).

This definition of the archeological gesture is consistent with Apichatpong's mysterious and poetic approach towards the violent repression of the historic memory of Thailand's northeast. For a series of questions traverse the entirety of the *Primitive* project: How to be contemporary to the villagers of Nabua and their numerous ghosts? How to share their dreams? How to film them? The co-presence with one's own present is not self-evident. It is rare and difficult, Agamben tells us, because it implies the constitution of an active relation with a part of the unlived that directly insists in the present. It is at this point that Apichatpong's aerial sensibility and his vivid conception of the dream come to play a decisive role in elaborating the archeological gesture that animates the *Primitive* project. For to summon ghosts without making them flee, to enter into resonance with the complex and entangled temporalities that co-exist in the present, *the filmic archeological gesture has to percolate the elusive*. The regression towards the past that he initiates aims not so much at restoring a traumatic primordial scene as letting past events modulate into new contemporaneities. An entire project of summoning that requires an art of tact, listening and allusion in order to bring to the surface not a distant past but something that could not be lived in another present. As Nabokov once wrote in *Transparent Things*: "A thin veneer of immediate reality is spread over natural and artificial matter, and whoever wishes to remain in the now, with the now, on the now, should please not break its tension film" (1989: 2). The archeological potential of the filmic dream courses through and rises up to precisely this thin veneer which envelops events lived, unlived and to be lived.

The movement of the dream that insists at the heart of the archeological gesture is not exhausted in the restoration of a historical positivity: it goes far beyond it, and below, taking up again "the first moment of freedom" until it coincides with the creative force of nature's passage that traverses the free "trajectory of existence itself" (Foucault 1984–85: 58, 60). Following such a trajectory implies the risk of a radical "derealization" as was suggested earlier. This derealization or decreation is something that we all experience to some degree in the face of Apichatpong's cinema. If Derrida was able to say that we need to learn to live with ghosts if we want to finally learn how to live, we can say that with Apichatpong, and his unique poetic manner of taking us to the heart of the Thai jungle and its war memories, we will learn to summon the ghosts of the past only to the same extent that we learn how to dream them. Part of the transparent and oneiric mystery of Apichatpong's cinema resides in the free movement of the dream and the way it has of tying itself to the future of the past.

In his recent seminars, Agamben likes to evoke the astonishing richness of the expression "to use" (*chresthai*) in ancient Greek. He particularly appreciates, it seems, the expression "to use (the) return", which in fact means "nostalgia". In the same vein, and at the margin of the archeological gesture, wouldn't "the use of going back and forth" be an appropriate way to evoke the blissful ambivalence of traveling through time – whether on board the spaceship of Nabua or not?

Notes

1. "The use of philosophy is to maintain an active novelty of funda-mental ideas illuminating the social system. It reverses the slow descent of accepted thought towards the inactive commonplace. *If you like to phrase it so, philosophy is mystical. For mysticism is direct insight into depths as yet unspoken.* But the purpose of philosophy is

to rationalize mysticism: not by explaining it away, but by the introduction of novel verbal characterizations, rationally coordinated"
(Whitehead 1968: 174, emphasis added).

2. "What is really 'in' experience extends much further than that which
    at any time is known. From the standpoint of knowledge, objects
    must be distinct; their traits must be explicit; the vague and unre-
    vealed is a limitation. *Hence whenever the habit of identifying reality
    with the object of knowledge as such prevails, the obscure and vague
    are explained away.* It is important for philosophic theory to be
    aware that the distinct and evident are prized and why they are. But
    it is equally important to note that the dark and twilight abound"
    (Dewey 1929: 20–1, emphasis added).

3. I refer here to the English work of mysticism from the fourteenth
    century, an anonymous guide to the contemplative life that defines
    darkness as "a lacking of knowing" to be entertained as such to
    make space for divine love (Anonymous 1922: 30). One can find a
    rather surprising echo to this classic of negative theology in a recent
    text by Graham Harman, published on the occasion of Documenta
    13. In "The Third Table" he prolongs in an openly mystical tone his
    object-oriented description of a non-sensual withdrawal of intel-
    ligible objects, affirming that "[t]he real is something that cannot be
    known, only loved" (Harman 2012: 12).

4. The theological acquaintance of the idea of self-enjoyment is under-
    lined in a luminous passage from *The Fold*: "Satisfaction as a final
    phase, as *self-enjoyment*, marks the way by which the subject is filled
    with its own data. This is a biblical – and, too, a neo-platonic – notion
    that English empiricism carried to its higher degree (notably with
    Samuel Butler). The plant sings of the glory of God, and while being
    filled all the more with itself it contemplates and intensely contracts
    the elements whence it proceeds. It feels in this prehension the *self-
    enjoyment* of its own becoming" (Deleuze 1993: 78).

5. See the seminar "Language, media and politics" (Agamben 2012),
    available from: https://www.youtube.com/watch?v=5tfv2Hmj6lE.
    For a rigourous discussion of the "dialectics of endarkenment" at the
    heart of Giorgio Agamben's thinking, see David Kishik, *The Power of
    Life: Agamben and the Coming Politics* (2012).

6. I am referring here to Lars von Trier's short "Defocus Manifesto"
    that belongs to a wider movement of resistance against the dic-
    tates of sharpness and storytelling. "The ultimate challenge of the

future – to see without looking: to defocus! In a world where media flock to kneel before the altar of sharpness, draining life out of life in the process, the defocusists will be the communicators of our era – nothing more, nothing less!" (Trier 2014: 473). Does the force of dreaming that traverses every shot of Apichatpong's cinema not in the end speak to an irreducible propensity to defocus?

7.   In another interview, a charmingly casual Apichatpong proposes a different version of the same anecdote: "In Buddhism, one does not really need cinema if one knows how to make use of our mind because our mind is the best projector in the world. Across the centuries, it accumulates an amount of untold stories – at least that's what Buddhism holds. [...] The trick is to know how to decode that which has been saved on your hard disk and I think that's what meditation does, or at least I believe. For further information, you can always ask David Lynch..." (Weerasethakul 2011), available from: http://www.universcine.com/articles/apichatpong-weerasethakul-le-cinema-tend-a-la-preservation-des-ames-et-notre-esprit-est-un-appareil-de-projection

8.   For a multifaceted, schizoanalysis-inspired exploration of the relation between cinema and neuroscience, see Pisters (2012).

9.   See Marc Menichini's (2012) "Apichatpong Weerasethakul Recalls His Past Films and Future Plans", available from: http://blogs.indiewire.com/criticwire/interview-apichatpong-weerasethakul-recalls-his-past-films-and-future-plans. The film to which Apitchapong refers has now been released: *Cemetery of Splendour*.

10. See, in this respect, Thomas Lamarre's remarks on the "soulful bodies" that populate Japanese animation films: "The soulful body is analogous to Deleuze's concept of the time-image" (Lamarre 2009: 312).

11. See Deleuze (1993: 11, 23): "Life is not only everywhere, but souls are everywhere in matter. [...] the whole world is only a virtuality that currently exists only in the folds of the soul which convey it, the soul implementing inner pleats through which it endows itself with a representation of the enclosed world."

12. This text echoes with remarkable clarity the theological regions of Whitehead's thought, taking as a starting point this marginal affirmation from *Modes of Thought*: "The account of the sixth day should be written, He gave them speech and they became souls" (Whitehead 1968: 41).

13. This is my translation from the French original (2002). This passage
    has been quite significantly changed in the English translation.
    Here is the new version of it (most probably re-written by Stengers
    herself): "The specificity of human experience is not defined by its
    limitations, but rather by 'leaps of the imagination" that respect no
    limitation. Of course, community of intuition still rules and even
    proliferates. But it may also be experienced as such. In addition, the
    entertainment of a new proposition is felt as an event" (Stengers
    2011b: 442).

14. In *Semblance and Event*, Brian Massumi offers an insightful per-
    spective on this question when he affirms that "proprioception is
    natively inventive. It is the body's in-born technique for the pro-
    duction of nonsensuous similarity. The body's automatic abstrac-
    tion method. [...] All techniques of existence bringing forth virtual
    events work with proprioception and its privileged connection with
    thought" (2011: 125).

15. About the "element of return at work in every becoming", see
    Frédéric Neyrat's book, *Homo labyrinthus: humanisme, antihuman-
    isme, posthumanisme* (2015: 162–6).

Works Cited

Agamben, Giorgio. "What is the Contemporary?". *What is an Appa-
    ratus? And Other Essays*. Stanford: Standford University Press,
    2009a: 39–54.

Agamben, Giorgio. *The Signature of All Things: On Method*. New York:
    Zone Books, 2009b.

Agamben, Giorgio. "Language, media and politics". Published
    March 18, 2012. Available from: https://www.youtube.com/
    watch?v=5tfv2Hmj6lE (accessed September 13, 2016).

Anonymous. *The Cloud of Unknowing* [*A book of contemplation the which
    is called the Cloud of unknowing, in the which a soul is oned with God*].
    London: John M. Watkins, 1922.

Apichatpong, Weerasethakul and Thunska Pansittivorakul. "A Conversa-
    tion with Apichatpong Weerasethakul". *Criticine*. Published April 29,
    2006. Available from: http://www.criticine.com/interview_article.
    php?id=24 (accessed Septemebr 12, 2016).

Apichatpong, Weerasethakul. "The Memory of Nabua: A Note on the Primitive Project". In: *Apichatpong Weerasethakul*. Ed. James Quandt. Vienna: Synema, 2009. 192–206.

Apichatpong, Weerasethakul. "Le cinéma tend à la préservation des âmes... et notre esprit est un appareil de projection." *Univers Ciné.* Published on February 17, 2011. http://www.universcine.com/articles/apichatpong-weerasethakul-le-cinema-tend-a-la-preservation-des-ames-et-notre-esprit-est-un-appareil-de-projection (accessed on February 16, 2016).

Blanchot, Maurice. *The Infinite Conversation*. Minneapolis: University of Minnesota Press, 1993.

Carrion-Murayari, Gary, and Massimiliano Gioni. Eds. *Apitchatpong Weerasethakul: Primitive.* New York: New Museum, 2011.

Cousins, Mark, and Tilda Swinton. "Two Letters". *Apichatpong Weerasethakul*. Ed. James Quandt. Vienna: Synema Publikationen, 2009: 7–12.

Deleuze, Gilles. *Cinema 2: The Time-Image*. Minneapolis: University of Minnesota Press, 1989.

Deleuze, Gilles. *Difference and Repetition*. New York: Columbia University Press, 1994.

Deleuze, Gilles. *The Fold: Leibniz and the Baroque*. London: Athlone Press, 1993.

Deleuze, Gilles. *Two Regimes of Madness*. Ed. David Lapoujade. New York/Los Angeles: semiotext(e), 2006.

Deleuze, Gilles, and Félix Guattari. *What is Philosophy?* New York: Columbia University Press, 1994.

Dewey, John. *Experience and Nature.* London: George Allen and Unwin, 1929.

Foucault, Michel. "Dream, Imagination, and Existence". *Review of Existential Psychology & Psychiatry* 19.1 (1984–85): 29–78.

Harman, Graham. "The Third Table". *Documenta 13: 100 Notes – 100 Thoughts, no. 85.* Ostfildern: Hatje Cantz, 2012.

Kim, Jihoon. "Learning about Time: An Interview with Apichatpong Weerasethakul". *Film Quarterly* 64.4 (2011): 48–52.

Kishik, David. *The Power of Life: Agamben and the Coming Politics*. Stanford: Stanford University Press, 2012.

Lamarre, Thomas. *The Anime Machine: A Media Theory of Animation*. Minneapolis: University of Minnesota Press, 2009.

Leutrat, Jean-Louis. *Vie des fantômes: Le fantastique au cinéma*. Paris: Cahiers du cinéma, 1995.

Loy, Mina. *The Lost Lunar Baedeker*. Ed. Roger L. Conover. New York: Farrar, Strauss and Giroux, 1996.

Massumi, Brian. *Semblance and Event: Activist Philosophy and the Occurrent Arts*. Cambridge: The MIT Press, 2011.

Menichini, Marc. "Apichatpong Weerasethakul Recalls His Past Films and Future Plans". *IndieWire*. Published on August 10, 2012. Available from: http://blogs.indiewire.com/criticwire/interview-apichatpong-weerasethakul-recalls-his-past-films-and-future-plans (accessed on February 16, 2016).

Nabokov, Vladimir. *Transparent Things*. New York: Vintage, 1989.

Newman, Karen. "A Man Who Can Recall His Past Lives". *Apichatpong Weerasethakul*. Ed. James Quandt. Vienna: Synema Publikationen, 2009 : 143–52.

Neyrat, Frédéric. "Se sauver. Éléments pour une nouvelles alliance du cinéma et de la philosophie". *Débordements*. Published on April 8, 2013. Available from: http://www.debordements.fr/spip.php?article170 (accessed on February 18, 2016).

Neyrat, Frédéric. *Homo labyrinthus: humanisme, antihumanisme, posthumanisme*. Paris: Éditions Dehors, 2015.

Pansittivorakul, Thunska. "A Conversation with Apichatpong Weerasethakul." *Criticine*. Published on April 29, 2006. Available from: http://www.criticine.com/interview_article.php?id=24 (accessed October 6, 2016).

Pisters, Patricia. *The Neuro-Image: A Deleuzian Film-Philosophy of Digital Screen Culture*. Stanford: Stanford University Press, 2012.

Quandt, James. "Push and Pull: An Exchange with Apichatpong Weer-asethakul". *Apichatpong Weerasethakul*. Ed. James Quandt. Vienna: Synema Publikationen, 2009: 182–92.

Rancière, Jacques. *The Intervals of Cinema*. London: Verso, 2014.

Sélavy, Virginie. "Uncle Boonmee: Interview with Apichatpong Weeras-ethakul". *Electric Sheep Magazine: A Deviant View of Cinema*. Published on November 13, 2010. Available from: http://www.electricsheep-magazine.co.uk/features/2010/11/13/uncle-boonmee-interview-with-apichatpong-weerasethakul/ (accessed on February 18, 2016).

Stengers, Isabelle. "Whitehead's Account of the Sixth Day". *Configurations* 13.1 (2005): 35–55.

Stengers, Isabelle. *Thinking with Whitehead: A Free and Wild Creation of Concepts*. Trans. Michael Chase. Cambridge: Harvard University Press, 2011a.

Stengers, Isabelle. *Cosmopolitics, vol. 2*. Minneapolis: University of Minnesota Press, 2011b.

Trier, Lars von. "Defocus Manifesto (Denmark, 2000)". *Film Manifestos and Global Cinema Cultures: A Critical Anthology*. Ed. Scott MacKenzie. Los Angeles/Berkeley: University of California Press, 2014: 472–3.

Whitehead, Alfred N. *The Concept of Nature*. Cambridge: Cambridge University Press, 1920.

Whitehead, Alfred N. *Modes of Thought*. New York: Free Press, 1968.

I believe that a film like *Tropical Malady* tries to imagine a world beyond the forms, substances and universal laws of scientific reason, and that this is accomplished not through time travel (obeying its penchant for universal definitions and reasoning) but from a revirtualization (in imagination) of time. *Tropical Malady* is a film that reinvents itself, almost spasmodically, starting from "something" that resembles travel, which returns even before coming, reintensifies itself elsewhere, and which I declare to be – perhaps in slightly too ceremonial a manner – time. I tried to study (ethologically speaking) what the film could be made, and remade, out of, by following its untimeliness, and not its spacing or gaps (which one might simply fill with being), but rather by emancipating it from what I call "the [universal, scientific] reason of the thinkable".

Indeed, that any resemblance between the two segments of the film, and its two protagonists proves impossible – that organizational structures and themes of efficient causality (before-after) are held in abeyance (by the unexplained passage between films) – convokes an entirely new ethics based on the "moods" of the aesthetic and its micro- or infra-components. In such a way that "other possible ways of knowing and doing can be contemplated without the charge of irrationality, mysticism, or idle fantasy".[1] "Ethology" is the word that I give to this contemplation that Denise Ferreira da Silva wishes for. Like her, and the poethical figures that she encounters in the works of Octavia E. Butler, I am interested in whatever undoes the fixity of Time and Space. It is an effort, or an attempt of the imagination – and no doubt that fabulation is at the forefront of such an undertaking.

There is a passage in Fred Moten's *In the Break* that is worth sharing, if only to complicate this matter of the return, of the Same, the Iconic, of that which appears to irreversibly re-present (itself). Here is what he writes:

Something slips through the cracks or cuts of iconicity, likeness, metaphor, such that thinking operates in the absence of any real correspondent and translational manipulation of the concept of internal similarity or pictorial internal relation. [...] The question, then, is how to describe that experience, and bound up in this question is the assumption (pointed to above, bitten off Wittgenstein) that description, rather than explanation, is the task with which we must now be concerned. More precisely, we must attempt a description of an experience whose provenance or emergence is not reducible to logical structure, pictorial internal relation or internal similarity; it is an experience of the passage or cut that cannot be explained because those formulations upon which our explanations must be grounded – spooky actions at a distance; communication between space-time separated entities; rigid, naturalized, but anti-phenomenal samenesses – are themselves so profoundly without ground. Like the strange correspondence between distant particles, like the mysteries of communication with the dead (or with tradition), the paradoxically elective and imperative affinities of and within ensemble are to be described within a radical improvisation of the very idea of description (in and through its relation to explanation), one that would move us from hidden and ontologically fixed likeness to the anarchization of variation, variation not (on) but of – and thus with(out[from-the-outside]) – a theme.[2]

There are many things to be pulled out of this quotation, but I would like to draw attention to the idea of an "anarchized" description and *variation* that leaves no chance or respite for generalized equivalences. In the cut, whether it be internal (to a film) or external (between films), something happens

and something "strange" occurs and is transmitted, in spite
of the irreversibly separated. It is the affinities, the bonds,
that are themselves strange. And how can we describe these
passages, these speeds (against aggressive deterritorializations
or explanatory accelerations)? It seems to me that each essay
in this book tries to describe in its own way how the variation
(and deformation) of an event is the effect of an outside more
distant than any form of exteriority, a passage that is irreducible
to any given symptom or symptomatic explanation. It is from
the outside that the variation of what we believe to be the same
operates. This outside – these intensive affinities – remains
inexplicable from the point of view of someone who records the
movement of variation's forces.

In a collaboration, in order to be able to make something
(through improvisation and/or composition), one must invest
in this *confidence from one to another*, this belief or this "love
supreme" as it is incarnated in one of John Coltrane's albums. In
the case of Apichatpong, I would go so far as to say that the film-
to-be-made participates in the construction (and continuation) of
a friendship, a bond, an attachment. Take *Cemetery of Splendour*:
the entire film is an ode, if not a love letter to Jenjira Pongpas.
She and Apichatpong have known each other for such a long
time that she is a part of his life (perhahps even his lives, the kind
that breathe life into his films). Each one of Apichatpong's films
is like a family portrait, or portrait of friends. There are things,
relations (between actors and directors, for example), alliances,
pacts and linkages that are undone more slowly than others,
and even some for which one would do anything to never have
to let them go. If one engages the question of irreversibility, one
quickly realizes that it is inseparable from the problems raised by
duration and the ephemerally given.

There are tendencies that cannot be reversed, but that is also
what defines us as provisional effects. Irreversible does not
mean eternal, let alone immortal. If our tendency is to endure

– but only with the transience this verb gives us – what is it that we hold dear, that moves us, which gives life, again? Who do we want near and be close to? What sort of surrounding or sociality do we want? What materials are our alliances made of? What is it that we care about? And my answer to each of these questions barely varies: that the world has the capacity to believe in us and establish mutual trust. That Apichatpong creates a cinema *out of love* (for a people, a person, for the cinema itself) is what touches me the most deeply and makes me want to write "with" him. I'm interested in that which creates or makes a link, beyond these notions of irreversibility and chronology.

I will always remember this story, told to me years ago by my father, about our neighbour, a real fan of television series who, in spite of passing years in front of her tiny screen, couldn't understand how a character who died in one series could be resurrected and survive in another,[3] before dying and coming back to life yet again. Clearly, she couldn't take as given or normal this (dis)continuity effect, even if death (disjunction) had already struck once. It's because the return of the same remains the exception to the rule. Thus, it is evident that a work of art has this wonderful, miraculous capacity to short-circuit common sense, the logic of the living and the dead, the logic of from-life-to-death. That is what the following study of *Tropical Malady* elaborates. It makes habits falter in order for a whole new series of perceptions, and even suspicions, to arise, so that, in the encounter, they can inspire other ways of speaking (to each other), touching (each other) and thinking (oneself). We must, just like Apichatpong, develop a sort of patience, a slow and rigourous pragmatism in front of something that we believe to be identical with something else.

M. NourbeSe Philip comes to mind and this sentence in particular: "Repetition drives the event and the memory simultaneously, becoming a haunting, becoming spectral in its nature."[4] Apichatpong's actors are those who, in the proper sense of the word, *haunt* his cinema relentlessly, exchange roles no matter their age, and repeat themselves in spite of having aged – irreversibly mortal. This is, among other things, what I wanted to describe in saying that his films are "dreams to be followed". Fantasies and ghosts that are at once to be followed and to be continued [*à suivre*]. For me, the friendship, the love, that I suspect between Apichatpong and his actors is at the centre of this haunting *and* this continuation (differentiation, dramatic variation), without which there would be nothing left to do.

Intercession invokes this differentiation. There is a sentence by Eunsong Kim that makes me think of Apichatpong's practice and mine: "You cannot do what I do because you do not love who I love."[5] The question of practices (of making) is entangled with a love that also needs to be made.

Notes

1. Denise Ferreira Da Silva. "Toward a Black Feminist Poethics". *The Black Scholar: Journal of Black Studies and Research* 44:2 (2014): 90.

2. Fred Moten. *In the Break: The Aesthetics of the Black Radical Tradition*. Minneapolis: University of Minnesota Press, 2003: 91–2.

3. M. NourbeSe Philip. *Zong! As Told to the Author by Setaey Adamu Boateng*. Toronto: The Mercury Press, 2008: 201.

4. Eunsong Kim. "Found, Found, Found, Lived, Lived, Lived". *Scapegoat* 9 (2016): 59.

Ronald Rose-Ántoinette

Of That Which Gives Life, Again

> I live from an underlying layer of feelings: I am
> barely alive
> *Clarice Lispector (2012: 19)*

It begins with a quotation by Japanese novelist Ton Nakajima, gracing the film's opening, that must be read as a warning ("We are all, by nature, wild animals. Our task as human beings is to become like the tamers who hold their animals under control and train them to do things that go against their bestial nature"), quickly followed by an image of outstanding cruelty. It is prefaced by a statement insisting as much on our "human nature" as our "task" of becoming human (at this point, one may fear that the film is an elaboration of this inaugural commandment) and, shortly after, with the meeting between a nameless, lifeless body, and a squad of armed soldiers who encircle it; a pale, cadaveric body strewn on the grass in the middle of a forest. There lies a dead body, yet the soldiers, all smiles, don't miss the opportunity to rejoice and delight as if all tragedy could be avoided. Nobody mourns the passing of this unidentified body (we never see the face of the victim) that one of the soldiers simply happened to "find". Each of them wants to be pictured, victorious, in the company of the cadaver; they smile and nobody moves. The photographic moment inserts itself into the cinematic flow of images. The photo's primary function is not to remember the deceased through a mnemonic technique that conjures up the forgotten; no, this photo that the soldiers take, and that we ourselves see being taken, is meant to capture the moment and archive the event to which they respond as present and alive. It is not death which precipitates their memory, but the life proper to them. They do not see human death, but the gaze of an other mixed up with theirs, the vision of the screen, the elective site of their attention.

The remains of the dead end up being carried on a stretcher. One of the soldiers, holding a walkie-talkie, attempts a radiophonic liaison with a woman with whom he has fallen in love. Yet the signal quality starts to fade; the speech of his interlocutor reaches him as a bunch of cryptic sounds. (For the temporality of a long-distance romance is bound to produce interferences that alter meanings and generate new ones.) Pop music starts to play. An individual, stripped naked, wanders through the image, partnered, it seems, with the landscape where the soldiers were seen. In any case, it is possible that the naked man and the armed soldiers never cross paths.

But still: a few minutes later, it begins yet again when the credits appear on top of one of the soldiers who, considering his presence on the screen, is surely aware of his being exposed. *Tropical Malady*: the title of the film, amidst an orchestra of crickets, fully reveals itself. Keng (Banlop Lomnoi), the soldier who falls in love before our eyes, maybe even for our eyes, feigns indifference for that which takes place behind or in front of this image without counter-shot (an image that assures the alterity of our intimidating gaze – us being the vision of the screen). This smile and this look, both mischievous, uncover us; we know ourselves to be seen, and even charmed. Or according to Didi-Huberman's formulation, "that which we see only gives – or lives – itself to our eyes by that which regards us" (Didi-Huberman 1992: 9). Keng's eyes can't be stopped from rolling and sweeping across the screen, stretching an erotic gaze between his world and the scene of our own projection. So reluctant to confront us, or even face us directly, his eyes move from one part of the shot to another, in order to better latch onto our existence which, as ghostly as it is, would not know how to succumb to indifference.[1] Their movement undoubtedly stems from the actor consciously playing his role, as they reinvest a sense of modesty and naivety that falsely departs from the narrative project. The soldier's hesitant attitude towards the camera lens goes as far as to raise suspicion about the fictive character of the work – it needs to be said that Apichatpong's protagonists occasionally take advantage of their roles to entertain the possibility of belonging to (and longing for) a film world, acknowledging the dreamlike quality and ghostly assemblage of their experience.

Appearing close to ten minutes after the first image, the credits bother (what appeared to be) the beginning of the film. But someone – or is it the film itself? – proclaims that an image has already-always started without us; that it is impossible for the force of change to begin and end *for us*.[2] Alas! Even though we took care to arrive on time (or was it before time?). But after all what, strictly speaking, constitutes a beginning? Is it true that cinematic art, in order to function, requires a human decision (and gaze)? And most of all, to what extent is it even necessary to ontologize traditions – being at the beginning/ beginning for being – when art can easily do without punctuality and measurement? Apichatpong's cinema never stops singing the refrain of a time liberated from volitional and individuated forms. One can agree with Guattari, channeling Nietzsche, and say: "Everything has to continually begin again from zero, at the point of chaosmic emergence: power of eternal return to the nascent state" (Guattari 1995: 94). For it is hardly after beginning that the film re-establishes a "point of emergence" that has been but also will be. And:

> As you can see, it's impossible for me to deepen and take possession of life, which is aerial, is my light breath. But I do know what I want here: I want the inconclusive. I want the profound organic disaster that nevertheless hints at an underlying order. The great potency of potentiality. (Lispector 2012: 20)

And if, wanting the inconclusive, we ricochet off the limit of thought, it is because we are struggling with the gravity of our finitude, of our held breath. So fugitive and exhaled is this life which Lispector perceives, that it leaves us with images "barely alive" and words barely finished, barely there. If the eternal didn't want the cut, if the cut didn't want the eternal singularity of time-without-time, we would continue to believe in the rarity or preciousness of things. And to think that by a feeling, if not an intuition, we dismiss the tragedy of apnea, exhaling the inestimable "potency of potentiality".

Neither beginning nor conclusion. All the less because: as Keng arrives at his beloved's home and begins to browse a photo album; as we witness the birth of a loving relationship between Tong (Sakda Kaewbuadee), a young man from the country, and the soldier (who ends up succumbing to his charms); and while nobody objects to their love affair – punctuated by long walks in the city and forest, ordinary enough of activities,[3] consisting as much of modesty as romantic clichés – the inexplicable makes itself felt.[4]

I say the inexplicable only because I want to account for a *cut* whose intervention into the stream of images can't be clarified, conditioning the start of an *n*th film, the establishment of an *n*th fabulation around a spirit that, wandering in the forest, torments its residents. A story of ghosts, of "wild animals". The story of a soldier who takes himself for a hero and hunts this demon capable of appearances equally strange and familiar in the meanderings of the jungle-night. It is the course of the film that finds itself deviated, most of all from its narrative tendency.

Thus we veer towards *A Spirit's Path,* following the appearance of the credits on top of a coarsely drawn tiger, in a becoming-painting of the screen (that oscillates with the drawing). By way of the cut, *A Spirit's Path* becomes Apichatpong's *n*th proposition, one inspired by a Noi Inthanon's short story[5], with Banlop Lomnoi and Sakda Kaewbuadee in the title roles. Except that, in this case, we land in the year of aphasia: since instead of assuming the roles they play during the first half of the work – which we can call *film 1* for the purpose of this study – the protagonists find themselves propelled to another level of action. The two men are no longer recognizable in the same way, neither to us nor to themselves. It is their excessive and omnipresent smiles from *film 1* that lie beneath the malicious traits of *film 2.*[6] It is *Tropical Malady* (*film 1*)'s pop sensibility that slides underneath *A Spirit's Path* (*film 2*)'s logic of predation. The possible is distributed otherwise. Enough for us to press for – in light of the reversal to which we bear witness, the positions that are activated, the antagonisms and (counter)tendencies that operate – an ethology of images.

Yet, the problem isn't to determine how we arrive at such a *détournement,* but to admit into our study the types of perception that it triggers, as Weerasethakul's words seem to entail: "In film, it's more of a gradual accumulation of feelings" (Kim 2011: 48). And as it feels increasingly, *a film* – indefinite from its own perspective – emerges. Certainly, the faces are not unfamiliar to us, but the shape of their encounter reshuffle the cards of our normal (habitual) modes of perception. We are called to be attentive to the ruse, to the new forces thrown into the defamiliarized bodies; the undressing of one revealing a tattooed body from head to toe. What anguish, what fright, fills the eyes of the naked man and the soldier once they are face-to-face for the *n*th time!

The paradox of the return is that they may have encountered each other twice, each occasion having also been the first; they haven't forgotten anything either since they are only, each time, discovering each other/themselves. One is not even the same in the eyes of the other, since it appears to have never been. "The forgotten thing appears in person to the memory which essentially apprehends it" (Deleuze 1994:140). The forgotten in the *n*th: how then to dissociate the before from the after if the principle of recognition applies to neither of them? The reappearance of their habitual modes of perception must necessarily be suspended: undoing the habit that we have contracted; contracting new ones; giving value to the variation of the performance. Vulnerable, neither seen nor known, is how the soldier and the naked man appear to their respective memories: it is by the cut that they essentially come into sight. Their meeting speaks for a time that neither comes before nor after, a time that attests to *this* encounter and not another one. Forgotten, that is how *Tropical Malady* appears, having fallen into the shadow of a block of amnesic images, "almost aphasic, now standing in the void, now shivering in the open" (Deleuze 1995: 9). It is time itself that doesn't remember anything, that opens beyond its personalizations and recollections. Only a singularity remembers – which is a way of saying that *one* remembers everything, but also nothing without being judged.

No doubt, it is an illness to believe in the return of individuated forms and subjects, and to believe in the universality of a lived perception. But it is an illness that needs to be overcome. As it is true that that which returns through the earth's centrifugal expression is not the same, or in other words identical, but a *dramatic variation*. That the cut resets the counter to zero and releases a new memory taking the already seen for the unseen, for something forgotten and unknown: it is without remembering the other that one appears, that one finds oneself apprehended, seized by the memory of the other. Recognition does not prevail since the event of archaic fixations is offset and because the film itself unarchives the memory of its previous occurrences. The dismissal of recognition parallels the dissolution of a measured time, one that is dictated by individuated forms and subjected to apodicted certitudes. Truth does not have to be unmasked, but in various ways, the mask meets the conditions for an affirmation of the multiplicity of being. Why would a thinker like Kierkegaard draw out two different trends of time (and its rehearsals)? Maybe because one would never be able to conquer the melancholia of existence without having to unleash its own prophecies. "Repetition and recollection are the same movement, just in opposite directions, because what is recollected has already been and is thus repeated backwards, whereas genuine repetition is recollected forwards" (Kierkegaard 2009: 3). Such that, in clear opposition to the retrogression of memory, the two men are called to *remember forwards*, that is to activate the differential element of their existence. And if, under the sting of the forgotten, nothing comes before and nothing comes after, it is because the cut, neatly executed, testifies to the contemporaneity of *films 1* and *2*. At the same time, that which has taken place coexists with that which will come into existence. At the same time, by way of the cut, the present has happened and has not happened yet, deprived of all clarity and instantaneity. In short, no time has passed between *1* and *2*. The cut could possibly be mistaken for a dividing line between a before and an after, but the fact of the matter is that through the absence of recognition between *films 1* and *2* it is the arrow of time that proves to be broken. To echo a well-known expression of Deleuze and Guattari, the cut here has the value not of lack but of desire.[7] A desire of and for itself; desiring desire, without any goal but to dissolve the beating of time. Thus it is neither with the past nor with the future that one needs to break, but with a certain habit that situates them on both sides of an agonizing present, exhausted of its potentialities, even though the latter has not stopped giving (or desiring) with its untimely figurations. Clarice Lispector's "I am barely alive," cited in the epigraph, is not to be confused with a person full of agony, but corresponds more closely to the more-than-aware singularity of an event equally unbearable as uncontainable by a subject.

That through which we pass – from *1* to *2* – is nothing but a temporal complex whose memory is integral to its proper break: a break with the usual, clichéd sense of time; with the need to submit each image to comparison, as if between them, in spite of them, the manufacturing of a narrative should occur, following a scheme of intelligible reduction. The passage from *1* to *2* (and vice versa since the ordering of efficient causality is a product of such reduction) enacts a type of "pseudo-narrative detour"[8] that leaves no dogma standing and no certitude binding their alliance. In passing (away, with, from, towards), the very meaning and necessity of an ethology of images emerges based on the attitudes and the affects that traverse them, rather than on their supposed sensory-motor liaisons.

If it seems difficult to understand the film's temporality based on a metric denominator, it is precisely because it obscures all definition or measure, and because the *tropicality of the spirit* and the *path of the malady* never stop modifying and implicating one another. We may try to add them up yet we must return to the cuts that each begin and end *with*. As long as it is, the film (but which film?) is always simultaneously and topologically more *and* less than we consciously determine. The reality of the film-during-the-film is there to remind us such elusiveness. For from the point of view of any beginning everything seems without precedence – anoriginally and indefinitely open.

Pragmatically speaking, our knowledge of the film, of its duration, is undermined the moment we pay attention to (and inquire about) its intensive qualities: we do not know how to delineate its contours as long as its lines continue to inform a cartography that does not begin nor end with our decision. It is, practically speaking, impossible to have a clear vision or understanding of its body. Any ethological study of the film, therefore, must admit a topology of latitudinal (according to this or that degree of intensity) and longitudinal (under this or that extensive set of relations) forces according to which the film exceeds and composes (with and beyond) itself. The telos of beginning-and-end is unworthy of the film's anexactitude, of its anti-narrative and anti-psychological singularizations.

Deformation of people, dissolution or involution of forms: it seems that in keeping from sacrificing the detours and the sentience of the event, Apichatpong facilitates the contemplation of a variety of existential styles that are unlocalizable with respect to a desubjectivized time. It is not that the stories have to be followed or told in a particular order but, rather, that a tale (which Apichatpong multiplies) guides us across a field of fugal/transversal experimentation, a *film-during-a-film*, to liberate the dramatic variations of speed between rhythmic becomings and appetitions of all sort. "Weerasethakul's unique compression of past, present and future defines a filmic present that encapsulates everything that has happened before as something that is happening again" (Joo 2011: 92). In spite of narrative development, the time of *Tropical Malady* is at once unlocalizable and ineffable.

Wherever, whenever: a film is a dream to follow and be continued. A film comes alive and vibrates in its own right, setting its precedent. All this to say that by deviating from the romantic narrative between the two men, Apichatpong does not pretend that it ends. For it continues, or could be continuing, along another trajectory, one that refuses the status and the identity of the present. *Film 1* could be the alternative to begin with (*+1*). The alternative never being anything but folded inside of the image, co-present in the actual regime of experience – refusing the dilemma (to choose) between a before and an after. The event takes place but the intensification continues elsewhere (otherwise), thus exceeding the finished image-concept and the narrative project. It is a matter of abolishing the individuality of the present: past-present and present-future coexist in the differential and transitional element of the cut.

That which goes on between the two regimes of images (+ *1*) affirms them both as alternatives and as manners of existence. This is how Apichatpong discovers an even richer life, more contingent and varied than one may think: triggering a series of micro-perceptions that look beyond (or below) the strictures of the actual to locate barely lived trajectories. As a result, Apichatpong's images of the everyday – the sort that appear during the credits of *film 1*, exemplified by fleeting shots of shopkeepers noticing the camera's presence – are always concurrent with (and transversal to) otherwise realities. At every occasion, Apichatpong assumes the right to disarm truth of its promontory authority.

✳✳✳

"I would like to remember the time when I was still in my mother's womb, but I don't have the concentration for that" (Weerasethakul 2009: 105). When and where did everything begin? Neither Weerasethakul, nor anybody else for that matter could know how to remember a life that was never entirely their own. This is a proposition that can be annexed to the fact that the beginning is a limit that Boonmee (from the eponymous film), ghost of his past lives, is unable to reach. And Boonmee's memory does not exhaust itself unless the possible withers away, and the faculty of vision reaches its proper limit, in a blind image ("What happened to my eyes? They are open, but I do not see anything"), and that thought comes up against its own confines, to the point of making memory impossible ("Here is where I was born, in a life that I no longer remember"). Thus, could there not be something unforgettable only in the broadest of lives, vaster than any immensity, any qualified extension? Could there not be something unforgettable only

in that which has not yet started; wherein the beginning, the birth, the start, never came? It is on the contrary everything that has been rendered possible which exposes itself to being forgotten. What memory is the most capable of, all things considered, is apprehending the lived as something forgotten and irrecoverable. A future, unforgettable.

> To call up the past in the form of an image, we must be able to withdraw ourselves from the action of the moment, we must have the power to value the useless, we must have the will to dream. Man alone is capable of such an effort. But even in him the past to which he returns is fugitive, ever on the point of escaping him, as though his backward turning memory were thwarted by the other, more natural, memory, of which the forward movement bears him on to action and to life. (Bergson 1991: 85–6)

If what "bears [one] on to action and life" can be called belief, it must undeniably be found in the conditions where we are ready to *contract* whatever necessary, to struggle for new spaces of thought, sensation and perception. One needs to have the temperament of a warrior – one that troubles the established values and moral codes that turn this world into an appearance and life into an anomaly. It is the ethic in which one must believe in order to pass from *film* to *film* without being dominated by an image of the past. Except that this passage effects a liquidation of a certain type of learning, the evisceration of certain ways of intervening in the past and selecting that which seems useful to our actual perception. Yes, perception must learn what it takes to acquire a habit![9]

> I am humble and don't without uneasiness awaken a past for a long time dead. Whatever knowledge they have of it, the livings do not possess the past as they believe to: if they think to hold it, the latter escapes

them. I give myself excuses: building my theory, I
didn't forget that it leads to a movement which is
elusive; I could situate only thus the sacrifice which is
incumbent upon us. (Bataille 1988: 133–4)

Staying as close as possible to this "movement" in which
Kierkegaard, Bataille and Bergson participate, we must now
ask how the ethical contraction that Apichatpong proposes is
conditioned by the runaway movement that agitates many of
his images.

Taking *film 1* for example: we are at Tong's workplace, an ice
factory where the images flow in intermittent manner, without
any explanation. We surprise the young man cutting a block
of ice, before he stands and directs his gaze off-screen; the
following shot frames a statue in the foreground depicting a
swan about to take flight. The background is populated by a
river lined with houses, a road, etc. The camera remains fixed,
punctuated by the occasional zoom. The worker is evacuated
from the profilmic field; the image only retains the constant
whine of the factory's ice cutting machines. A swan, a river, a
riverbank, houses, cars, trees, the sky: nothing extravagant or
beautiful in this image of a banal byroad apparently so trivial
that it only makes sense to itself. How could the image teach us
anything about the psychological state of the character, when
Tong's gaze exhausts itself and merges with the image (the shot
ends with a fade to black), in its elementarity (muddy water, a
milky sky, the earth, a riverbank whose meaning we know not),
and its vivacity (everything is in movement, including the swan
"caught" in his tracks, and the slicing of the ice sawing away
off-screen)? *Tropical Malady* (*films 1* and *2*) is laced with details,
gestures of this type, images filled with ineffability, opening onto
indeterminacy, without precise direction.

Or this other scene from *film 1*, where Tong's dog watches
over his master sleep in a hammock. The animal is caught in

anticipation, ears perked, ready to… Ready for what, all things considered? Neither man, nor dog is determined to move; one sleeps while the other watches. And yet, all we try to imagine is the movement that could lead one or the other to move in one way or another. Image at zero intensity, animated by a degree of irresolution. What will it do? What will happen to it? What the animal is capable of, we do not know. But how long (this) perception is! To wait or anticipate. But wait for or anticipate what? That is how much the sign of the image is on the verge of unraveling.

It's the entire Weerasethakul-operation that is a counterpointed un-telling, interspersed with various channels – in fugal composition – like so many pathways or subterranean plans. A number of the "pseudonarrative" digressions in *Uncle Boonmee Who Can Recall His Past Lives* exemplify how each of Apichatpong's films is offset by some other story: a fugitive buffalo returns to his master, a photographer is caught in a becoming-monkey, a deceased spouse reappears at dinner time, a princess and a catfish are sexually coupled, a ghost (re)appears, Boonmee dies (again), burning red eyes sparkle, a monk births his own doppelgänger, and so on… Such is the force (and the cut-up style) of the pseudo-narrative deviation: to thwart our need for efficient causality. Even in the interior of each story emerges an adventure, an alternate route, inhabiting and multiplying points of view. Each line establishes itself as the blueprint of another one, each point of view as the milieu of an alternative thrust.

✳✳✳

A soldier mourns in verse (and song) at the end of *A Spirit's Path*: "At present, it is myself that I see. Mother. Father. Fear. Sadness. All of this has been so real, so real, that it has given me life." But what is this "it" to which the man refers? What is this *it* "so real" that is for him the breath of life even when faced with the threats of a tiger? One would think that it was for him, as for Lispector, to live "from an underlying layer of feelings", to be barely alive, barely there. And that he never knew how to live life (and never could), having long since wandered in the jungle like a ghost of the future, of the past, who never had the chance to feel the fear nor the sadness of being incarnated. That is exactly why the experiential unconscious (*it*) is at once father, mother and orphan, generativity of all generations (illegitimate and non-causal). It is also why the indefiniteness of *that* which gives life, as much as it is made of the tiger, trees, people, and cosmos that innervate his vision, is without memory of anyone or anything.

> Becoming is that which literally evades, flees, and escapes mimesis, whether imitative or reproductive ("Mimicry is a very bad concept"), as much as *memesis*, both mnemonic and historical. Becoming is amnesic, prehistorical, aniconic, and sterile: it is difference in practice. (Viveiros de Castro 2014: 159–60)

How could we doubt for even a moment that a life has always preceded us, and always passes us by? How could we doubt that a lifeline runs through the self, exceeding all beginnings and endings of subjective existence? Nothing is *self*-evident, and life is in no way reducible to a few well-ordered traits or behaviours. The becoming in the *it* is not made in anyone or anything's image, or to please anyone, and without any historical generalization. This is what the cut from *+1* to *2* exemplifies (the becoming of *a* film – left undefined "in practice" – is itself "amnesic" and "prehistorical": an image without an image, that is to say without memory). This is also what the soldier in *A Spirit's Path* admits with an emotion that makes felt the importance and intensity (the *so* contained in the *so real*) of a life that is given to him. That is to say, by the vigorous passage of that which remembers nothing and thus gives life (this "difference" that Viveiros de Castro speaks of), the latter finds himself in the vertiginous moment of a life barely lived.

***

The force of the image against the reason of the thinkable: we have not sufficiently underlined to what extent Apichatpong's cinema serves an *indefinition* of the present, working in the immediacy of the relation between past and future, and the extent to which his films enact a time-without-time, that is to say a *passage*, an emotion entirely exempt from beginning or end. To say it in the manner of Duchamp, this passage is "infrathin": the delay between pastness and futurity can *barely* be isolated.[10] And if *Tropical Malady* calls forth a thought of the infrathin, perhaps it is because the film inspires a trans-apparitional practice of the image – of an *image for the making*, to be assembled from the middle of what defeats the distribution and evaluation of time. A thought that transforms itself into the equivalent of an ethical act, an act of faith: not in the hereafter, but in a *life during life*, contemporary (and not posthumous) to this life. Indeed, nothing stipulates that individuality is the site of a dream or the epicentre of a life. It is in this vein that Whitehead can write: "Life lurks in the interstices of each living cell, and in the interstices of the brain" (Whitehead: 1978: 105–6). And it is in this vein that Apichatpong never stops splitting his characters apart, situating them outside of themselves, beyond true and false, like when the monk in *Uncle Boonmee* sees the man who he has been in spite of who he will be, all in the very same moment. As if time itself lives according to a mode of *interstitiality* and *ghostliness*, far from homeostatic equilibrium, irreducible to any given cell or individualized image. Apichatpong's modes of existence, even when they enter into strange relations, bow to the necessity – the innocent necessity – of an in-between where they oscillate and eclipse one another.

At once terrifying and inspiring: an effect *can* precede its cause.

The *making* of time: is it not that which Apichatpong's images look towards? Beyond the labor of re-membering and dis-membering.

But how to extract a sensibility from the force of change? How to give life to "the moving web of time," to take up Didi-Huberman's formulation (Didi-Huberman 2002: 273)?[11] We understand here the difficult challenge of the film that Apichatpong is committed *to make*: channelling this inordinate time-without-an-image, that "in order to become visible, 'seeks bodies and everywhere encounters them, seizes them to cast its magic lantern upon them' " (Deleuze 2008: 13).[12] There is no cause for concern about the fact that Apichatpong invents so much time to create his images: a duration, even an eternity, but an eternity that needs to be conceived no matter what. The image (and the so-called narration that compliments it) becomes the flight plan (a slow eternal detour) of a time-passage which can only be made – as long as there is a desire for and especially from it. The time of images, thus desired by Apichatpong, breathes entanglement and indefinition, so that we cannot say exactly where we land, or where we stop to rest, as brief as such a pause may be. At least, if we were to read Whitehead's cosmology through Lispector's ode to life, we could argue that every time we say "now" or "I live" we create nothing but a plane of experimentation, *trying* to get a hold of that which is all too elusive.

> Life is the enjoyment of emotion, derived from the past and aimed at the future. It is the enjoyment of emotion which was then, which is now, and which will be then. This vector character is of the essence of such entertainment. The emotion transcends the present in two ways. It issues from, and it issues toward. It is received, it is enjoyed, and it is passed along, from moment to moment. (Whitehead 1968: 44)[13]

Apichatpong's images and situations never fail to underline that experience is beholden to this emergence ("from" and "towards") that Whitehead houses under the notion of – at first sight, personalized – emotion. If the past never ceases to be, but continues to haunt, it must also be said that the future is never quite exempt from a present that ceaselessly moves in it, and "that the same 'now' both ends [the reader's] past and begins his future" (James 2003: 42). But in what, and why, should we rejoice if we live more in/of these entanglements than in/of a categorical present? Maybe because the experience of passage (whose terms must not be given in advance and violence) is tantamount to the creative emotion that defends us from all individual isolation. Because passages are the only points of view, the only realities that prevail under the beam of an *aesthetic of the earth*: de-touring (with, away, from, towards) itself. In fact, in light of Apichatpong's propositions, we must reshape this idea of emergence as laid out by Whitehead, and fostered by James: one cannot help but see that *Tropical Malady* gives a sense of emergence that is not as straight and unilinear as it sounds in the latter quotes. With respect to Apichatpong's time-images, provenance and aim do not belong to any apprehension (or region) of time. Future-past, transversibly and indefinitely desired: a movement must be experimented in order to arrive at their limit.

To restore this ante-linear passage: there is no better way to conceive Apichatpong's artistic trajectory, his manner of constructing (with his own) refrains. Arnika Fuhrmann's claim about Keng and Tong's homosexual desire, as one that comes against the normative enactments and rehearsals of time, through its ordinary rendition and "noncoherent quality," can't be emphasized enough (Fuhrmann 2016: 131). With *Tropical Malady* it is the image of time (of its re-production) that is queered out by a love relationship that belongs neither to a before (as primitive) nor to an after (postponed as a threat), but is expressed outside the beating of time.

"A vagrant now and again" (Delany 1994: 20, 79):[14] this is the sort of refrain that makes science-fiction heavyweights like Samuel R. Delany, who want to capture that all too elusive and ephemeral pull from the faintest light at the end of the tunnel, a must-read alongside films like *Tropical Malady*. Apichatpong never renounces the idea of a time that is essentially floating and entangled, implying the coexistence of a past that is no longer and a future that is not yet with an open, undefined present. "In the singularity of paradoxes," affirms Deleuze, "nothing begins or ends, everything proceeds at once in the direction of both past and future" (1990: 80). The force and singularity of the journey, not in time, but of time itself, is to know how to "pass-ify" and "futurize" itself all at the same time, to not give itself as such. But is not emotion, or the "with" in the *com*-plex, the only indefinitely multiple (non)sense of "at the same time"? Apichatpong best articulates this idea through the character of Boonmee (a dreamer, or someone who remembers his own future anterior, which the film title refers to as "lives"), or even through the amorous/hateful relationships in *films 1* and *2*. The problem of sense (as tendency) in Apichatpong's work is not reducible to a contradiction, it is before all else paradoxical, struck with (e)motion.

✳✳✳

I find the following passage in Georges Bataille's *Inner Experience*: "Experience is, in fever and anguish, the putting into question (to the test) of that which a man knows of being" (Bataille 1988: 4). And I realize, in a transversal reading of Bataille, that it is in sweat and wonder that the soldier of *film 2*, after having crawled in a style contrary to his human nature, has no other option but to confront the tiger whose spirit he stalked; that it is in the dangerous proximity between feline and soldier, both immersed in a night of ecstasy, that what it means to be human is put to the test. It's that, suddenly, the animality of the soldier is skittishly linked to the tigerly eloquence of the spirit. The tiger's language enters into a process of transduction (of fabulatory subtitling, similar to the monkey who addresses himself to the soldier earlier on), wherein it instructs the human to surrender. There are no lips to read or interpret, only flowing voices that collide and distort.

But who considers themselves human and who considers themselves animal in this story? It's a deceptive situation. To be honest, I do not know if the word "reversibility" refers as adequately as possible to this transition of animality, but nevertheless I can assert that a real indeterminacy concerning each body's position on the spectrum of living flesh erases the anthropological division that would invalidate the perspective, the *by-path*, or the *by-way*, of the tigerly human. Apichatpong's intercession, or shamanism, ecstatically rises up against such a "bifurcation of nature" [15] in a final sequence that mutually implicates the spoken reality of the animal and the bestial becoming of the soldier. The moral injunction of the film's opening scene, attributed to the Japanese novelist, fades before the night, before the beast, before the indeterminacy of the soldier's speech and subjection. And I say "indeterminacy", not only because the night becomes feline, but because it is also solar. This can be seen quite clearly in *Tropical Malady*'s epilogue, where the greenery of the treetops recedes into the dawning of a new day, coupled to the unveiling of another night.

> Even though I grew up in a small town where the land is flat, there were strange animal sounds in a quiet night not unlike those up on the hills. The tales and the landscapes were imprinted in my mind. I always imagine a parallel world with these elements, one where I did not physically live. When I had a chance to make films, which in itself is to create another world, I always resorted to this jungle. The love and fear of mysterious darkness and jungle became my addiction, along with filmmaking. (Weerasethakul in Quandt 2009: 225)

A condition, a request from and for cinema: that the day is eclipsed for the duration of an image, a dream, of a ghostly existence. But one essential question remains: where to place the limit between day and night if not in a contrast,[16] in a passage liberated from systematic and formal pretentions? How and where can one make an image of a time-without-time, that is, an image without beginning or end, if not from the "mysterious opacity" of a vitality – albeit it a ghostly vitality – irreducible to the conventions of perception? Accordingly, the untranslatability of the monkey and the tiger's speech, in spite of the words they are endowed with, may be simply a symptom of their anoriginary entanglement. Fabulation – if the term is susceptible enough to this kind of spooky-*talk*-at-a-distance – is an essential part of the human/non-human junction, and the nurturing of their mutual opacity. There is no difference to reduce, no strangeness to elucidate/see through the motif of a higher *ap*prehension.

> In this version of understanding the verb to grasp
> contains the movement of hands that grab their
> surroundings and bring them back to themselves.
> A gesture of enclosure if not appropriation. Let our
> understanding prefer the gesture of giving-on-and-
> with that opens finally on totality. (Glissant 1997: 91)

Transparencies (relations to the self) are abbreviations of a trans-forming world. But if we insist on the creation of difference, from difference (as departure), it is because the only way to succeed in doing so is to remain concerned with the ineffable (that is untranslatable) share that eludes the empire of the possible. If we already think of the passage as a way of getting across, of overcoming two differences, as with a password for instance, we miss a tremendous opportunity: that of generating something else – more and less than a vessel. Opacity is the attitude that must guide us once we take Apichatpong as an intercessor. Wrapped in nocturnal noise, I cannot bring this surround, this dream that is Apichatpong's cinema back to me ("my hands"). I do not pretend to understand it, or explain it (to myself). I have a sympathy for it (a "giving-on-and-with") that aims to prolong the wonder, the love and the fear of the mode of opacity that Apichatpong practices. The trajectory of this text – strewn with deviations – refuses to evaluate his work on the "scale of transparency" (Glissant 2011: 14) desired and instituted by Western philosophies. Yet, I see Apichatpong's cinema as one that creates an interesting friction with the ideas and propositions that have travelled with me; one that troubles and, at the same time, parallels the signifiers that have hitherto dominated the context of my thinking process. Though I do not want to place his films before the horizon of transparency drawn by European onto-epistemologies, I deeply desire their encounter in order to unleash *something* that may intimidate my perception of, and belief in the theories that have shaped the stage of the return. I see Apichatpong's cinema as one that may allow us to imagine a greater outside to the forms and images that have currency in the spaces which have (more or less successfully) disciplined the intellectual life of many contemplators of time, including me. If it seems hospitable to the ideas prompted and promoted by a Eurocentric (predominantly white, male) cohort of thinkers, it nonetheless interrupts or halts their transcendental legitimacy by provoking these limits and cuts that exhort us/ them to think *again*. So we don't go straight, we only begin to open on the totality of the world. Neither a confirmation (of) nor in conformation (with), his cinema, as experience, that is, as *thought*, puts into test the onto-epistemological resistance of what I think-"I"-know of being and becoming. In other words, the unsettling of perception cannot be done without taking the propositions or ideas that one lives with (and is haunted by) somewhere else – finding the alternatives with-in. As the writer and filmmaker Trinh T. Minh-ha so eloquently claims, the only attitude that is worth pursuing is one that allows us to *speak nearby*, by adventure and creativity.

***

Apichatpong is a time-*maker* in the sense of appreciating and dramatizing its untimeliness. Time (of history, of survivance, of becoming, of the night-jungle) and images knot themselves in an experiential fabric with the figure of the ghost, that which leaves and yet comes back, that which haunts without being any less real and capable of (inter)action. However they appear (as effects of the film-dream[17]), Weerasethakul's ghost-travellers are unable to come to life ("now and again") without having to *pass away* (from and towards). The gaze of the soldier that repeatedly provokes the camera during the opening credits of *Tropical Malady* (*film 1*) calls the time of the image into question: perhaps it evokes his embarrassment, barely concealed, of addressing himself to us or seducing us as his ghost counterparts, after having erased or complicated all screenic distance. Perhaps we, as well, (will) have passed away! But: "From where, from what place and what time, does this ghost speak to us?" (Didi-Huberman 2002: 32). If a "truly 'historical' rendition," proposed by Nietzsche "would be ghostly speech before ghosts" (2007: 242) how then could we avoid thinking that it is through this quality – spectrality – that Boonmee addresses those who come to visit him ("What if I'm already dead?" he asks, anxious about his passing); that it is in the ghostly manner and contemporaneous presence of those who are no longer or not yet living that Apichatpong haunts – the image of – time?

Hence Didi-Huberman's question: "Can we ever *foresee* that which, of the past, is called to *survive* and haunt us in the future?" (Didi-Huberman 2002: 512), a question that I modify as follows: How to think and feel that which from today haunts – already – the hypothetical tomorrow? And how will we recognize that which from our "vagrant now" will be "called" to err "again"? Only the force of change (with its fabulatory variants and infrathins) can trouble the categories of repetition and recognition, and offer an opportunity to marvel at the art of variation. And only one sole eternity – not just of a Nietzschian type, for we also need to project ourselves into the activity and the technicity of the detour – can "see" that which could have defeated memory's terrifying act of forgetting. But, to think about it for a moment, do we want to persist in the present of those who will inherit ours? Not only must modes of fugitivity be parasitic towards (protest against) that which petrifies us (and prevents us from dreaming), but also become the architects of an innocent love. This is what Boonmee's wife, Huay, seems to suggest to her beloved one: "Ghosts aren't attached to places, but to people. To the living."

So: what if we're already alive?

Notes

1. Didi-Huberman adds: "Inevitably there is a split that separates in us that which we see from that which sees us. One must start from this paradox where in unfolding, the act of seeing opens itself in two" (Didi-Huberman 1992: 9). For Didi-Huberman, it is essential to follow Maurice Merleau-Ponty towards an inevitable Visibility. For more on this subject, see the chapter "The Intertwining – The Chasm" in Merleau-Ponty's *The Visible and the Invisible* (1968).

2. Nietzsche's hypothesis of the eternal return is splendidly expressed by Zarathustra's speech in "Of the Vision and the Riddle": "From this gateway Moment a long, eternal lane runs *back*: an eternity lies behind us. Must not all things that *can* run have already run along this lane? Must not all things that *can* happen *have* already happened, been done, run past? ...And are not all things bound fast together in such a way that this moment draws after it all future things? *Therefore* – draws itself too?" (Nietzsche 1969: 179).

3. An air of the quasi-quotidian, the quasi-documentary, floats around their peaceful romance, to the point where the recording of the images and sounds intrude on their intimacy. And the image of the soldier, accompanying the credits, who returns our look, seems to be embarrassed by the presence of the camera. It's here that one of the main themes that is noticed by critics appears: the strange

naturalism and familiarity of the images. Thus, for Claire Valade, the way that Weerasethakul mixes the fantastic and the quotidian "as if it was totally natural" serves to discredit his realism and not "attach himself", when on the contrary, in the eyes of Natalie Boehler, the film "cultivates a sort of naturalism of the supernatural" that begs to be celebrated (302). See Claire Valade's "Oncle Boonmee (celui qui se souvient de ses vies antérieures): la vie dans l'entre-monde" (2011) and Natalie Boehler's "The Jungle as Border Zone: The Aesthetics of Nature in the Work of Apichatpong Weerasethakul" (2011).

4. A note on the subject of the inexplicable is warranted, in that it fails to induce its proper erasure in the infra-empirical order. It does otherwise: nothing can account for this essential difference that crucially cuts within the plane of the image-body. The (sensuously) explicable cannot be thought as its negative, or its impossibility, as that which it most fiercely opposes. Furthermore, it's the inexplicable that produces the shock of images, and not the inverse. "It is not surprising that, strictly speaking, difference should be 'inexplicable'. Difference is explicated, but in systems in which it tends to be cancelled; this means only that difference is essentially implicated, that its being is implication. For difference, to be explicated is to be cancelled or to dispel the inequality which constitutes it" (Deleuze 1994: 228).

5. Noi Inthanon is the pen name of Malai Chupinit, author of *Long Phrai: Suea Kueng Puthakan* (1955) from which the Thai title of the film, *Satpralat*, is taken: literally "monster".

6. One must not be deceived by the numbering that sequences the film's passing. One and two, but we can also count one and one and… in order to underline the eternal beginning of what we experience in perception.

7. Desire being the leitmotif of *Anti-Oedipus*.

8. Guattari specifies that one of the aims of this detour is a *"dispositional mise-en-scène, a bringing-into-existence, that authorizes, 'secondarily', a discursive intelligibility"* (Guattari: 2008: 26). This "bringing into existence" is what we call trans-apparition, the metamorphosis of subjects or things that participate in a situation (movement) that is far from equilibrium.

9. We believe that it is this twisting of habit that defines Weerasethakul's way of fighting for a broadening of feeling, and that

the passion of his images are complicit in a defamiliarization with those that preceded them.

10. "In Time the same object is not the same after a 1 second interval" (Duchamp 1983: note 7).

11. It is our perceptions that do not last long enough to glimpse even one process of individuation whose movement through form takes all of the time afforded to it. The speed of perception is a matter that the philosophy of the future must endow with new books and theories.

12. Here, Gilles Deleuze builds on a passage from Tome I of Marcel Proust's *In Search of Lost Time*.

13. Life is enjoyment: which means that it is nothing other than activity, and not simply passion. Whitehead writes according to this form of transcendental empiricism, which undoubtedly brings him close to a thinker like William James. "Each moment of experience," he writes, in a style that sympathizes with the ideas of James, "confesses to be a transition between two worlds, the immediate past and the immediate future" (Whitehead 1967: 192).

14. This refrain appears multiple times in *Flight from Nevèrÿon*, Middletown: Wesleyan University Press, 1994. Delany is a writer that doesn't know where and when to begin. Another groundbreaking work of afro-speculative fiction is *Kindred* by Octavia E. Butler: the story takes us to the core of this complexity, beyond the strictures (historical, scientific) and formulations (necessities, determinations) of time.

15. Here I put forth my own interpretation of this Whiteheadian syntagm. We can read in *The Concept of Nature* that such a dismembering of reality "bifurcates nature into two divisions, namely into the nature apprehended in awareness and the nature which is the cause of awareness. The nature which is the fact apprehended in awareness holds within it the greenness of the trees, the song of the birds, the warmth of the sun, the hardness of the chairs, and the feel of the velvet. The nature which is the cause of awareness is the conjectured system of molecules and electrons which so affects the mind as to produce the awareness of apparent nature" (Whitehead 1964: 30–1). It seems to me that Weerasethakul, just like Whitehead, disobeys the subjectivist principle of separation between appearance and reality, and looks to delve into an immediacy of consciousness, an immanence where human perception can no longer

distance itself from anything. The opacity of the Weerasethakulian gesture is reluctant to put the perspective of the so-called feline at odds with that of the so-called human. The fact is that the tiger not only knows how to think for himself, but also, and maybe most of all, makes think his felt surrounding. The essential aspect of the Weerasethakul-operation is not to bifurcate reality, but on the contrary, affirm the plurality of dialects and rationalities.

16. The *night-time* – a chance, that is to say a trigger that allows cinema to attempt to amplify the real – is directly put together through Apichatpong's (physical, photochemical) seizures: a necessity that goes to the length of appearing on the catalogue cover of one of his installation entitled *For Tomorrow, For Tonight*.

17. Apichatpong suggests that cinema, just like spectres and even dreams, is metamorphic in essence: "Film is like an entity by itself. The phantom is not disappearing but something that transforms itself. Cinema also has been transforming itself. Thus cinema can be a phantom in this sense: because it's something that you really need to dream. Cinema is a vehicle we produce for ourselves and as part of us. It's like an extension of our soul that manifests itself" (Kim 2011: 52).

Works Cited

Bataille, Georges. *Inner Experience*. Trans. Leslie Anne Boldt. Albany: State University of New York Press, 1988.

Bergson, Henri. *Matter and Memory*. Trans. Nancy Margaret Paul and W. Scott Palmer. New York: Zone Books, 1991.

Boehler, Natalie. "The Jungle as Border Zone: The Aesthetics of Nature in the Work of Apichatpong Weerasethakul". *ASEAS – Austrian Journal of South-East Asian Studies* 4.2 (2011): 290–304.

Delany, Samuel R. *Flight from Nevèrÿon*. Middletown: Wesleyan University Press, 1994.

Deleuze, Gilles. *Difference and Repetition*. Trans. Paul Patton. New York: Columbia University Press, 1994.

Deleuze, Gilles. *Nietzsche and Philosophy*. Trans. Hugh Tomlinson. London and New York: Continuum, 2002.

Deleuze, Gilles. *Proust and Signs*. Trans. Richard Howard. London and New York: Continuum, 2008.

Deleuze, Gilles. "The Exhausted". Trans. Anthony Uhlmann. *SubStance* 24.3, no. 78 (1995): 3–28.

Deleuze, Gilles. *The Logic of Sense*. Trans. Mark Lester with Charles Stivale. Ed. Constantin V. Boundas. New York: Columbia University Press, 1990.

Didi-Huberman, Georges. *Ce que nous voyons, ce qui nous regarde*. Paris: Éditions de Minuit, 1992.

Didi-Huberman, Georges. *L'image survivante. Histoire de l'art et temps des fantômes selon Aby Warburg*. Paris : Éditions de Minuit, 2002.

Duchamp, Marcel. *Marcel Duchamp, Notes*. Trans. Paul Matisse. Boston: G.K. Hall & Company, 1983.

Fuhrmann, Arnika. *Ghostly Desires: Queer Sexuality & Vernacular Buddhism in Contemporary Thai Cinema*. Durham: Duke University Press, 2016.

Glissant, Édouard. "Edouard Glissant in Conversation with Manthia Diawara." *Nka: Journal of Contemporary African Art* 28 (2011): 4-19.

Glissant, Édouard. *Poetics of Relation*. Trans. Betsy Wing. Ann Arbor: University of Michigan Press, 1997.

Guattari, Félix. *Chaosmosis: An Ethico-aesthetic Paradigm*. Trans. Paul Bains and Julian Pefanis. Bloomington/Indianapolis: Indiana University Press, 1995.

Guattari, Félix. *The Three Ecologies*. Trans. Ian Pindar and Paul Sutton. London and New York: Continuum, 2008.

James, William. *Essays in Radical Empiricism*. Mineola, New York: Dover Publications, Inc., 2003.

Joo, Eungie. "Present Again". *Apichatpong Weerasethakul: For Tomorrow For Tonight*. Ed. Maeve Butler. Dublin: Irish Museum of Modern Art, 2011.

Kierkegaard, Søren. *Repetition and Philosophical Crumbs*. Trans. M.G. Piety. Oxford: Oxford University Press, 2009.

Kim, Ji-Hoon."Learning about time: An interview with Apichatpong Weerasethakul". *Film Quarterly* 64.4 (Summer 2011): 48–52.

Lispector, Clarice. *Água Viva*. Trans. Stefan Tobler. New York: New Directions Publishing, 2012.

Merleau-Ponty, Maurice. *The Visible and the Invisible*. Ed. Claude Lefort. Trans. Alphonso Lingis. Evanston: Northwestern University Press, 1968.

Nietzsche, Friedrich. *Thus Spoke Zarathustra*. Trans. R.J. Hollingdale. Middlesex: Penguin, 1969.

Nietzsche, Friedrich. *Twilight of the Idols*. Trans. Duncan Large. Oxford and New York: Oxford University Press, 1998.

Nietzsche, Friedrich. *Human, All Too Human: A Book for Free Spirits*. Cambridge: Cambridge University Press, 2007.

Quandt, James. Ed. *Apichatpong Weerasethakul*. Vienna: Synema Publikationen, 2009.

Valade, Claire. "Oncle Boonmee (celui qui se souvient de ses vies antérieures): la vie dans l'entre-monde." *Séquences: la revue du cinéma* 270 (2011): 50–1.

Viveiros de Castro, Eduardo. *Cannibal Metaphysics: For a Post-Structural Anthropology*. Trans. Peter Skafish. Minneapolis: Univocal Publishing, 2014.

Weerasethakul, Apichatpong. "Ghosts in the Darkness." *Apichatpong Weerasethakul*. Ed. James Quandt. Wien: Vienna: Synema Publikationen: 104–17.

Whitehead, Alfred North. *Adventures of Ideas*. New York: The Free Press, 1967.

Whitehead, Alfred North. *Nature and Life*. New York: Greenwood Press, 1968.

Whitehead, Alfred North. *Process and Reality*. New York: The Free Press, 1978.

Whitehead, Alfred North. *The Concept of Nature: The Tarner Lectures Delivered in Trinity College November 1919*. Cambridge: Cambridge University Press, 1964.